D1744672

QUALITY OF LIFE

AND

HUMAN WELFARE

Proceedings of the Third Royal Scottish

Geographical Society Symposium

edited by

M. Pacione

and

G. Gordon

GEO BOOKS

NORWICH

Cover: Landsat image of Scotland, reproduced courtesy of
Nigel Press Associates Ltd.

ISBN O 86094 142 6

Published by Geo Books
              Regency House
              34 Duke Street
              Norwich NR3 3AP
              England

Contents

List of Figures

List of Tables

List of Contributors

Dr. F.A. Boddy

Director, Social Paediatric and Obstetric Research Unit, Greater Glasgow Health Board and University of Glasgow

Mr. M. Danson

Department of Social and Economic Research, University of Glasgow

Dr. T.R.B. Dicks

Senior Lecturer, Department of Geography, University of Strathclyde, Glasgow

Dr. G. Gordon

Senior Lecturer, Department of Geography, University of Strathclyde, Glasgow

Professor G.M. Howe

Department of Geography, University of Strathclyde, Glasgow

Dr. D.P. Milne

Microbiologist, Clyde River Purification Board, East Kilbride

Dr. I. Moffatt

Lecturer, Department of Environmental Science, University of Stirling

Dr. M. Pacione

Senior Lecturer, Department of Geography, University of Strathclyde, Glasgow

Mr. A. Robertson

Assistant Director of Housing Management, Scottish Special Housing Association, Edinburgh

Professor G.T. Stewart

Department of Community Medicine, University of Glasgow

Professor U.A. Wannop

Head, Department of Town and Regional Planning, University of Strathclyde, Glasgow

Mr. K. Yates

Senior Executive Officer, Strathclyde Regional Council, Glasgow

Preface

The theme Quality of Life and Human Welfare provided the focus for a symposium organised by Professor G.M. Howe, Dr. M. Pacione and Dr. G. Gordon of the Department of Geography, University of Strathclyde, on behalf of the Royal Scottish Geographical Society. The meeting, convened on 30th April 1982 in Glasgow, was attended by representatives from a wide range of organisations, including the academic community and local government agencies. This broad-based expression of interest reflected the widespread concern over quality of life in the modern world.

The symposium comprised three interrelated sections dealing with the broad subject areas of deprivation, housing, and health; with particular attention given to contemporary conditions in West Central Scotland. The nine major papers are presented in this volume, together with an introductory essay on the definition and measurement of quality of life, and brief comments by the discussants.

Publication of the symposium proceedings allows a larger audience to consider the papers presented, and hopefully will stimulate further discussion of and scientific enquiry into quality of life issues which are of relevance will beyond the confines of the urban-industrial environment of West Central Scotland.

The views expressed in individual papers are those of the authors and do not necessarily represent those of their affiliated institutions, the editors or the Royal Scottish Geographical Society.

George Gordon
Michael Pacione

July 1983

Chapter 1

The Definition and Measurement of

Quality of Life

Michael Pacione

INTRODUCTION

Concern over the quality of modern life is a characteristic of contemporary society. The meaning of the phrase 'quality of life' obviously differs a good deal as it is variously used but, in general,
it is intended to refer to either the conditions of the environment
in which people live (air and water pollution or poor housing for
example), or to some attribute of people themselves (such as health
or educational achievement). One of the reasons for the growing
interest in this field is the 'paradox of affluence' in modern
societies in which concern over the quality of life has seemed to
increase proportionately with technological progress and increases
in income. People in developed countries have come to realise that
'quality of life' is not necessarily a simple function of material
wealth. Growing awareness of the social, political and environmental health of a nation has led to the search for indicators,
other than those based on Gross National Product, which will more
adequately reflect the 'overall health' of a nation and the well-
being of its citizens.
    This paradoxical situation in which Western societies currently
find themselves may be explained, in part, by reference to Maslow's
(1954) hierarchy of needs model. According to this, in an industrial society individuals struggle for survival with limited time
for leisure, hard work is a virtue and wealth accumulation becomes
the ultimate goal of endeavour. The same may be said about the pre-
industrial situation of much of the developing world today. In the
transition towards a post-industrial society people can 'move beyond their basic concerns of living to a humanistic concern for what
living is all about'. The same theme is expounded in economic terms
by Wingo (1973) who states that there is a point in the course of
economic development when public attention shifts away from the
adequacy of private consumption toward more qualitative collective
satisfactions. At earlier stages the primary task of an economic
system is to produce to satisfy basic human needs - food, clothing,
shelter, medical care and education - and to increase the economy's
capability for doing so in the future. When most basic needs are
taken care of, however, an economic system can begin to address the
preferences of its consumers for more discretionary goods and services. Included in these is a set which make up the 'quality of
life'.
    Recent years have seen a rich harvest of quality of life pole-
mics in industrialised countries around the world. In his 1970

State of the Union address President Nixon remarked that 'never has
a nation seemed to have had more and enjoyed less'. A few months
later the U.S. National Goals Research Staff acknowledged that 'a
seemingly new concept has been added to the list of national goals.
The search for quality of life and the appeal for re-ordering the
national priorities embody the essence of this new aspect'. An increasing number of nations including U.S.A., Britain, West Germany,
France, Canada, Norway, Sweden and Japan are now producing social
reports or related compendia of social statistics as complementary
information to the earlier reports on economic trends. Concern is
especially intense in Japan where a special government survey on new
problems of advanced societies recently observed that 'the desire
for higher *quality* of life, which is a phenomenon common to all developed countries of late offers much to ponder about given the past
continuous growth in *quantity*'. The Japanese dilemma is highlighted
by the fact that between 1960 and 1970 gross national product per
head quadrupled, exports quintupled and the number of passenger cars
increased eighteenfold, for a population that grew by only 11 per
cent. But simultaneously the number of neurotic patients more than
trebled, land prices increased fivefold, and pollution and congestion grew much worse. Similar problems have been reported in
Western Europe and North America (H.M.S.O., 1977; Ward, 1980).

THE DEFINITION AND STRUCTURE OF LIFE QUALITY

Early studies of life quality were mainly concerned with defining
the meaning of the concept (Whitman, 1971; Dalkey and Rourke, 1973;
Hornback and Shaw, 1973; Wingo, 1973). According to Dalkey and
Rourke (1973) 'quality of life' means a person's sense of well being,
his satisfaction or dissatisfaction with life, or happiness or un-
happiness. Little additional insight is provided by Burton's (1977)
statement that quality of life is an elusive concept which relates
to something transcending the material concerns of everyday life.
    Some economists have maintained that it is possible to use con-
ventional economic indicators to measure quality of life. Merriam
(1968), for example, is of the opinion that in industrialised countries 'the level and distribution of income provide the most useful
overall measure of welfare that has yet been devised'. For Singer
(1972) the basic indicator of a high quality of life is to have as
much money as possible left over after taking care of the basic
necessities and to have the necessary time and opportunities to
spend it in a pleasant way. One of the major disadvantages of a definition of quality of life based on what amounts to the possession
of wealth is that the crucial psychological dimension is ignored.
This deficiency was acknowledged by Wingo (1973) who suggested that
quality of life may be reflected jointly in two dimensions: 1) the
income or wealth which represents command over physical resources
and is transferable and 2) the psychological inputs which are personal non-transferable and related to the intensity of private subjective gratifications. Accordingly most subsequent work concentrated a greater degree of attention on the individual's perception
of their material status in defining 'quality of life'.
    More recent investigations have advanced from pedagogic defin-
ition of life quality to identification of the major components of
the concept. In addressing this question there are two obvious ways
of determining the elements of life quality. The first is to derive
them from theory in psychology or sociology (Laswell and Kaplan,
1950; Maslow, 1954; Dahl and Lindblom, 1963; Fletcher, 1965;
Runciman, 1966; Stagner, 1970). The problem here is that despite
certain similarities in the views expressed, there is no generally
accepted social theory setting out the precise conditions

unambiguously defining human well-being, along with their relative weights. The second method is to ask people how they view their own state of well-being, thus attempting to discover by direct enquiry the elements on which this state depends. There has been considerable interest in the direct monitoring of quality of life via survey research in recent years (Kreiger, 1969; Allardt, 1973; Abrams, 1973; Andrews and Withey, 1976) but as Smith (1977) points out this has not yet reached the stage at which it could form a basis for definitive lists of criteria except for restricted populations. It is to be doubted, however, whether such a generalised goal of providing a definitive list of life concerns other than at a disaggregate level is either practical or desirable. The costs of direct measurement using large questionnaire surveys has generally deterred policy makers and academic researchers alike, with the result that attempts to identify major life concerns have turned to less direct methods. A third approach containing elements of both those outlined above is to refer to 'expert opinion' or the judgements of scientists and representatives of public views. Some examples of this Delphi technique are provided by the work of Dalkey and Rourke, 1973; Powell, 1973; Koelle, 1974; Molnar and Kammerud, 1975; and Jackson, 1975. The obvious disadvantage here is that these people may not truly represent the concerns of the population at large. There is no real evidence to show that the preferences and priorities of politicians and professionals resemble those of people in general (Hall, 1972; Lansing and Marans, 1969).

One guideline to what fundamental aspects of society should be isolated as important components of life quality is simply that the set of indicators chosen must be broad enough to include all the most important life concerns of the population whose well-being is being investigated. Moser (1970a) has suggested that the components of a good or happy life may defy measurement, but most people if asked to list the things in life which concern them would include 1) having enough to eat, 2) being healthy, 3) being housed in a congenial environment, 4) achieving work satisfaction, 5) having sufficient leisure, 6) personal security against crime. As Cantril (1967) stated 'the vast majority of people's hopes and fears revolve around the complex of personal well-being, and this is rather simply defined: a decent standard of living, a happy home life, better educational facilities'. In a more detailed statement Drewnowski (1974) proposed that an individual's well-being could be measured by an index composed of 1) nutrition, 2) clothing, 3) shelter, 4) health, 5) education, 6) leisure, 7) security, 8) social environment and 9) physical environment (Table 1.1). Bunge (1975) recognises eight different kinds of quality of life indicators; 1) physical, e.g. water quality, 2) biosocial, e.g. health and housing, 3) psychological, e.g. job satisfaction, 4) technical, e.g. percentage of skilled workers, 5) economic, e.g. income distribution, 6) social, e.g. welfare services, 7) political, e.g. participation in decision making, and 8) cultural, e.g. opportunities for continuing education. Smith (1973) on the basis of a review of literature on social indicators and social problems felt able to identify 'some general criteria of territorial social well-being'. These referred to seven major conditions, 1) income, wealth and employment, 2) the living environment, 3) health, 4) education, 5) social order, 6) social belonging, 7) recreation and leisure. Pacione (1980) in an investigation of the differential quality of life in a metropolitan village set out to identify those life concerns that were commonly held, that are relatively broad in scope, and that have some significant impact on people's sense of well-being (Table 1.2). By examining thirteen British and American studies of life quality he identified five life concerns or domains common to all studies, i.e. 1) housing, 2) health, 3) job, 4) standard of living and 5) leisure time. In addition four others were represented in two-thirds

Table 1.1 Composition of Drewnowski's level-of-living index

1. Nutrition (food intake)
   a. Calories intake
   b. Protein intake
   c. Per cent of non-starchy calories

2. Clothing (use of clothes)
   a. Cloth consumption
   b. Footwear consumption
   c. Quality of clothing

3. Shelter (occupancy of dwellings)
   a. Services of dwellings
   b. Density of occupation
   c. Independent use of dwellings

4. Health (health services received)
   a. Access to medical care
   b. Prevention of infection and parasitic disease
   c. Proportional mortality ratio

5. Education (education received)
   a. School enrolment ratio
   b. School output ratio
   c. Teacher pupil ratio

6. Leisure (protection from overwork)
   a. Leisure time

7. Security (security assured)
   a. Security of the person
   b. Security of the way of life

8. Social environment (social contacts and recreation)
   a. Labour relations
   b. Conditions for social and economic activity
   c. Information and communication
   d. Recreation: cultural activities
   e. Recreation: sport and physical exercise

9. Physical environment
   a. Cleanness and quietness
   b. Public amenities in the neighbourhood
   c. Beauty of the environment

   Source: Drewnowski (1974).

4

Table 1.2 Life concerns identified in a range of quality of life studies Investigations

Domains	S.S.R.C. March 1971	S.S.R.C. November 1971	S.S.R.C. December 1973	S.S.R.C. May 1975	Andrews and Withey, May 1972	Campbell et al., 1976	Consistency rating
1. Housing	x	x	x	x	x	x	6
2. Neighbourhood	x	x	District	x		x	5
3. Health	x	x	x	x	x	x	6
4. Job	x	x	x	x	x	x	6
5. Financial situation	x	Standard of living	x	x	x	x	6
6. Leisure	x	x	x	x	x	x	6
7. Family life	x	x		x	x		4
8. Friendships					x	x	2
9. Education	x		x	x			4
10. Police courts				x			1
11. Welfare services				x			1
12. Marriage	Marriage						3
13. Religion	Religion						1
14. Being a housewife	Being a housewife						2
15. British democracy	British democracy		x	x	National government	x	5
16. Town			Town				2
17. Financial situation			Financial situation				3
18. Life in Britain			Life in Britain				3
19. National economic and social policy					x		1
20. Self efficacy index					x		1
21. Amount of fun					x		2
22. Spare time activities					x	Things to do with family	1
23. Consumer index					x		1

of the listings. These were 1) the community, 2) family life, 3) national government, 4) education. For this study indicators of perceived local environment and expected standard of living in five years time were also employed since statements of domain satisfaction are primarily a reflection of the perceived gap between the individual's sense of his current situation in the domain and his aspirations concerning his position in the domain.

The close similarities among many of the listings provides guidance on the relative importance of various life concerns. Housing, health, employment and standard of living, for example, are key elements of everyone's definition of life quality. The sum total of these individual life concerns adds up to the quality of life, though it must be noted that the particular value or weight attached to each of the components varies from person to person and between social groups (Cantrill, 1965; Andrews and Withey, 1976).

THE MEASUREMENT OF QUALITY OF LIFE

It is clear from the foregoing discussion that any definition of life quality must include two fundamental elements 1) an internal psycho-physiological mechanism which produces the sense of gratification, and 2) external phenomena which engage that mechanism. Thus there is growing acceptance among policy makers and many in the social science community that two quite distinctive types of quality of life indicators are appropriate for measuring societal and individual well-being. The first comprise objective indicators characterised by hard measures describing the environments within which people live and work. These can deal with issues such as health care provision, crime, education, leisure facilities, and housing. Typical of studies using objective indicators is Liu's (1976) report on conditions in metropolitan U.S.A., and the Urban Institute's comparison of American cities (Flax, 1972). The second are subjective indicators intended to describe the ways people perceive and evaluate conditions existing around them. Work with subjective social indicators has been reported in Gurin, Veroff and Feld (1960); Bradburn (1969) while more recent studies based on national survey data have been carried out by Andrews and Withey (1976), and Campbell, Converse and Rodgers (1976).

As well as the objective-subjective distinction, quality of life indicators may also be classified according to their degree of specificity or generality (Figure 1.1). This refers to the proportion of the life space of an individual or group to which a particular indicator is relevant. For example, one subjective indicator may be concerned with a quite specific experience such as the quality of local shopping facilities while another may be concerned with a more general type of experience such as satisfaction with one's community. At the most general level an indicator may be related to evaluations of one's overall life. Objective indicators will also vary in level of specificity ranging, for example, from the quality of the interior fittings in a house to the availability of public facilities in the locality.

For geographers, the areal scale of reference is of equal importance. While the emphasis of social and economic statistics has always been on the state of the nation as a whole, geographers such as Smith (1973, 1977); Harvey (1972) and others, have demonstrated the even greater relevance of regional urban and intra-urban spatial variations in social conditions. Thus, among the basic problems in the development of quality of life indicators are the selection of a geographical unit of analysis and specification of the areas of concern for which measures are to be developed. To this may be added the problems of measurement reliability and validity. These

6

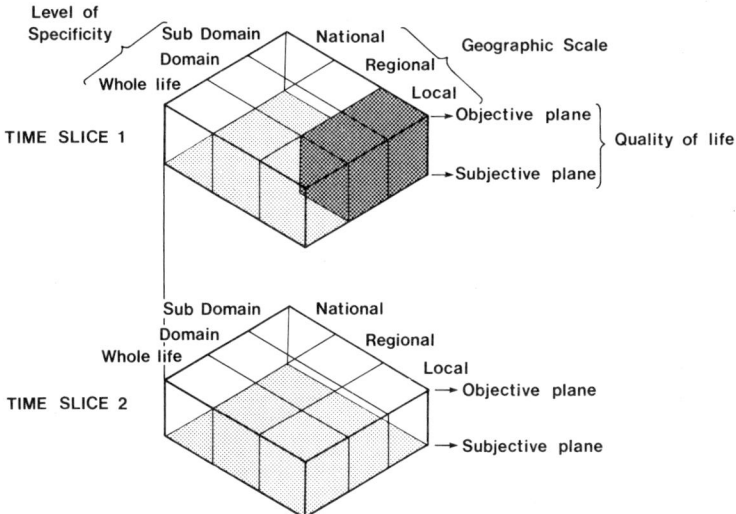

Figure 1.1 A four-dimensional structure for quality of life
            investigations

issues are discussed at greater length elsewhere (Pacione, 1982).

Objective Measures of Quality of Life

Empirical measurement of the quality of life in the U.S.A. was first
attempted, at the state level, in the 1930s but was not widely acknowledged until the work of Wilson (1967). Wilson adopted the criteria established by President Eisenhower's Commission on National
Goals to develop quality of life indexes, and assessed the life
quality for each state on nine components - status of individual,
equality, democratic process, education, economic growth, technological change, agriculture, living conditions, and health and welfare. Indexes for each of the components were constructed either by
simple linear aggregation or by more sophisticated factor analyses,
and the states were ranked accordingly. Several states such as Iowa
and New Jersey have also produced their own annual reports on quality of life. In addition a growing number of studies have attempted
to describe and explain differences in the quality of life between
cities e.g. Thorndike (1939, 1940); Bullard and Stith (1974); Lowry
(1970); Flax (1972); Flaming and Ong (1973); Coughlin (1973); Lineberry et al., (1974).
        All of these studies employed the objective or physical approach
by which secondary data or statistics are collected, organised, computed and analysed. One of the most ambitious investigations along
these lines, to date, is Liu's (1976) work on the quality of life in
243 U.S. metropolitan areas containing 139.4 million residents or
almost 70 per cent of the 1970 U.S.A. population. The cities were
divided into three groups according to population to produce 65
large SMAs (with populations of 500 000+), 83 medium sized SMSAs
(200 000 - 500 000) and 95 small SMSAs (with less than 200 000 population). The components of overall quality of life consisted of
five goal areas (Economic, Political, Environmental, Health and
Education, Social) broadly defined to 'cover most major concerns of

7

all individuals' (Liu, 1976). Each component was measured by a range of selected variables with a total of 123 objective indicators being employed. Liu's work, despite raising a number of operational and conceptual questions (Pacione, 1982), represents a monumental statistical task in collecting, organising, analysing and presenting quality of life factors for all of the major U.S. metropolitan areas and can be acknowledged as a valuable step forward in the social welfare field.

Subjective Measures of Quality of Life

While there is widespread agreement that purely economic indices provide an inadequate statement of general welfare, for some writers the need for other kinds of indices could best be satisfied by developing further sets of objective indicators; for others the need is for subjective data bearing on the meaning of objective conditions for the people actually experiencing them.

In the same year as Liu (1976) published his statistical analysis of objective measures of quality of life in U.S. metropolitan areas two equally comprehensive studies were produced which used subjective indicators to ascertain the quality of American life (Andrews and Withey, 1976; Campbell, Converse and Rodgers, 1976). Among the objectives of the research carried out by Andrews and Withey (1976) was to construct a battery of items (indicators) which would be modest in number, broad in coverage, of substantial validity and which would provide a statistically efficient means of assessing perceived life quality in the diverse domains (life concerns) most important for predicting people's general satisfaction with their lives. These important reports helped to redress the imbalance which existed in favour of objective studies of quality of life.

The use of subjective quality of life indicators has drawn criticism from some observers who regard them disparagingly as 'soft' measures of indeterminate meaning. This unfavourable image of subjective indicators is based on the belief that measurement error is a far more serious problem for subjective measures of well-being than for objective ones (who has ever heard of soft facts!). Both types of indicator, however, are prone to measurement error, and the relative accuracy of objective indicators can easily be overestimated (Campbell and Converse, 1972).

In general it is probably true that the majority of objective indicators are somewhat 'harder' than most of the subjective measurements in the particular sense of being more readily replicable or 'reliable'. However, if we are interested in indicators of human welfare measurement reliability is only half the picture. There is also the critical question of measurement validity or the fit between what is being measured and the substantive interpretations to be placed upon the measurement. Across the full range of purely objective indicators there is wide variation in the relevance or validity for the measurement of well-being. Some common indicators such as real income may require very little inferential leap between the entities they measure and conclusions as to their significance for well-being. It seems likely, however, that this leap is very substantial for the vast bulk of objective indicators generated by government agencies. The first report (March 1970) of the Urban Institute on the quality of life in metropolitan Washington, which compared social conditions in the capital with those in sixteen other large U.S. cities, illustrates this point. In this study quality of life in a community depends heavily on what the authors describe as social disintegration, citizen participation, community concern, and racial equality; but can these be measured adequately by, respectively, known narcotics addicts per 10 000 population,

8

voting turnout, contributions per head to charity appeals, and unemployment rates? This has led some researchers, such as Abrams
(1973), to conclude that 'The more one considers these concepts the
more one is persuaded that the way forward lies not in adding more
measures of conventional hard statistics, but rather in supplementing
the existing ones by adding in a clear cut way a new dimension to
the definition of quality of life - a dimension of the satisfaction
(happiness, contentment, psychological well-being, etc.) felt by
those who constitute the community and are the final consumers of
society's output of goods and bads and therefore the best judges of
society's performance'. Bateson (1972), Dalkey (1972) and Campbell
and Converse (1972) support this viewpoint in their contention that
the traditional measures of life quality form only a limited indication of the sum of satisfactions that make life worthwhile.

Thus researchers are often faced with the difficult choice between objective indicators of high measurement reliability but of
low validity for the purposes of assessing human welfare and subjective indicators whose measurement reliability is lower but whose
validity is much higher. In fact there is probably enough hetero-
geneity within the set of indicators of either type, where properties
such as reliability and validity for well-being estimates are concerned, that most debates presuming some generalised superiority of
one set over the other are simplistic and, in the final analysis,
quite sterile (Campbell and Converse, 1972). Such considerations
favour an eclectic posture that calls for the joint use of both
types of indicators. Despite this, subjective assessments of quality of life have not been employed to anything like the same extent
as those based on conventional hard social indicators.

THE RELATIONSHIP BETWEEN OBJECTIVE AND
SUBJECTIVE QUALITY OF LIFE INDICATORS

Most social indicator work has focused on either subjective or objective measures. A limited number of efforts have been made in recent years to collect both types of indicators within the same
study based on the belief that one type of indicator can contribute
to the interpretation of the other (Knox and MacLaran, 1978). A
fuller understanding of the meaning of objective health statistics,
for example, would be facilitated by complementary data covering
people's perceptions of their own health, the care they receive, or
the health services available to them. Given this it is intuitively
appealing to assume that there is a relationship between objective
and subjective indicators. Empirical evidence to date generally
shows the extent of correspondence between objective and subjective
indicators of the same phenomenon to vary from a strong relationship
(Campbell et al., 1976) to one in which it is weak or non-existent
(Schneider, 1975; Stipak, 1977). Given the complex nature of cog-
nition, however, it is hardly surprising that there should be diver-
gence between perceived conditions and conditions measured by means
of objective indicators (Pacione, 1982). Furthermore, the existence
of a simple direct relationship between objective and subjective
measures of life quality would clearly render one or other type of
indicator superfluous, just as the absence of such an association
reinforces the arguments for employing both types.

CONCLUSION

The geographer's major contribution to quality of life research, to date, has been the introduction of a spatial dimension in their work on objective territorial social indicators. This is important since in recent years there has been a growing awareness of the territorial bases of inequality in society, and policies designed to eliminate or ameliorate these inequalities have assumed explicit spatial dimensions (Gittus, 1976; House, 1977; Smith, 1977; Herbert and Smith, 1979). Since most people, even in todays mobile societies, spend most time in their home area (Perloff, 1969) and experience the benefits and disadvantages of their own localities it may be argued that areally based measures of life quality are not merely a product of the geographer's peculiar perspective on the general social indicators movement but are a necessary and logical extension of any realistic system of social reporting. From a geographical viewpoint an 'ideal' distribution of resources is one that is in direct proportion to the needs of areas. Clearly, however, such a pattern of territorial justice (Davies, 1968) between a set of administrative areas does not necessarily imply a situation of social justice among individuals within the areas. The danger lies in the ecological fallacy of attributing average conditions in any area to an entire population. This trap remains a necessary evil of the spatial or territorial approach to the study of quality of life; the larger the unit of enquiry the greater the potential ignorance of internal variations from the mean position.

Since assessments of social well-being or quality of life can be effective only if one is willing to recognise and deal with the complexity of social reality it could be argued that, in spatial terms, this means a move towards research at smaller geographical scales as indicated in Figure 1.1. Descriptive pattern identification and mapping may be of value at the larger scale as a pointer to detailed work but policy relevant quality of life indicators are more likely to be derived at the local area scale. Such indicators are also likely to be concerned with specific life domains, such as housing conditions, employment and health. The varied papers in this volume directly investigate some of these key components of life quality.

REFERENCES

Abrams, M. 1973. Subjective social indicators. *Social trends,* 4, 35-50.

Allardt, E. 1973. About dimensions of welfare: an explanatory analysis of a comparative Scandinavian survey. *Research group for comparative sociology,* Report 1, Helsinki University.

Andrews, F.H. and Withey, S.B. 1976. *Social indicators of well-being-Americans perceptions of Life Quality,* (New York).

Bateson, G. 1972. *Steps to an ecology of the mind.* (San Francisco).

Bradburn, N.M. 1969. *The structure of psychological well being.* (Chicago).

Bullard, J.L. and Stith, R. 1974. Community conditions in Charlotte 1970. *The Charlotte-Mecklenburg community relations committee,* (Charlotte N. Carolina).

Bunge, M. 1975. What is a quality of life indicator. *Social Indicators research,* 2, 65-79.

Burton, R. 1977. Leisure and the social services, in H.M.S.O. *Leisure and the Quality of Life: a report on four local experiments.* (London).

Campbell, A. and Converse, P.E. 1972. *The human meaning of social change.* (New York).

Campbell, A., Converse, P.E. and Rodgers, W.L. 1976. *The quality of American life.* (New York).

Cantril, H. 1965. *The pattern of human concerns.* (New Brunswick).

Cantril, H. 1967. *The human dimension: experience in policy research.* (New Brunswick).

Dahl, R.A. and Lindblom, C.E. 1963. *Politics, economics and welfare.*

Dalkey, N.C. 1972. *Studies in the quality of life: delphi and decision making.* (Lexington Mass).

Dalkey, N.C. and Rourke, D.L. 1973. The delphi procedure and rating quality of life factors, in *Experimental assessment of delphi procedures with group value judgements.* (Rand Corporation California).

Drewnowski, J. 1974. *On measuring and planning the quality of life.* (The Hague).

Flaming, K.H. and Ong, J.N. 1973. A social report for Milwaukee: trends and indicators. *Milwaukee urban observatory.* (Milwaukee Wisconsin).

Flax, M.J. 1972. A study in comparative urban indicators: conditions in 18 large metropolitan areas. *The Urban Institute.* (Washington D.C.).

Fletcher, R. 1965. *Human needs and social order.* (London).

Gittus, E. 1976. Deprived areas and social planning, in D.T. Herbert and R.J. Johnston *Social areas in cities,* 2, 209-233.

Gurin, G., Veroff, J. and Feld, S. 1960. *Americans view their mental health.* (New York).

Hall, P. 1972. Forecasting the quality of life in Europe. *Department of Geography Occasional Paper* 20. (University of Reading).

Harvey, D. 1972. Social justice in spatial systems, in Peet, R. Geographical perspectives on American poverty. *Antipode monographs in social geography,* 1, 87-106.

H.M.S.O. 1977. *Leisure and the quality of life: a report on four local experiments.* (London).

Herbert, D.T. and Smith, D.H. 1979. *Social problems and the city.* (London).

Hornback, K. and Shaw, R. 1973. Toward a quantitative measure of the quality of life, in U.S. Environmental Protection Agency. *The quality of life concept.* (U.S. GPO Washington D.C.).

House, J.W. 1977. *The U.K. space.* 2nd Edition, London.

Knox, P.L. and MacLaran, A. 1978. Values and perceptions in descriptive approaches to urban social geography, in D.T. Herbert and R.J. Johnston *Geography and the urban environment.* 1, 197-247.

Koelle, H.H. 1974. An experimental study on the determination of a definition for the quality of life. *Regional Studies,* 8, 1-10.

Kreiger, M.H. 1969. Social indicators of the quality of individual life. *Institute of Urban and Regional Development Working Paper 104.* (University of California Berkeley).

11

Lansing, J.B. and Marans, R.W. 1969. Evaluation of neighbourhood quality. *Journal of the American Institute of Planners,* 35(3), 195-99.

Laswell, H.D. and Kaplan, A. 1950. *Power and society: a framework for political enquiry.* (New Haven Conn.).

Lineberry, R., Mandel, A. and Shoemaker, P. 1974. *Community indicators: improving communities management.* (University of Texas, Austin).

Liu, B.C. 1976. *Quality of life indicators in U.S. metropolitan areas: a statistical analysis.* (New York).

Lowry, M. 1970. Race and socioeconomic well being: a geographical analysis of the Mississippi case. *Geographical Review,* 60, 511-28.

Maslow, A.H. 1954. *Motivation and personality.* (New York).

Merriam, J.C. 1968. Welfare and its measurement, in Shelon, E. and Moore, W. *Indicators of social change: concepts and measurements.* (New York).

Molnar, D. and Kammerud, M. 1975. Developing priorities for improving the urban social environment - a use of delphi. *Socioeconomic Planning Sciences,* 9, 25-30.

Moser, C.A. 1970a. Some general developments in social statistics. *Social trends,* 1, 7-11.

Pacione, M. 1980. Differential quality of life in a metropolitan village. *Transactions of the Institute of British Geographers.* New Series 5(2), 185-206.

Pacione, M. 1982. The use of objective and subjective measures of life quality in human geography. *Progress in Human Geography,* 6(4), 495-504.

Perloff, H. 1969. A framework for dealing with urban environment: introductory statement, in Perloff, H. *The quality of the urban environment.* (Resources for the Future Inc. Washington D.C.).

Powell, A.G. 1973. Methodology in the strategy for the North West region with special reference to evaluation. *Proceedings of PTRC Seminar on urban and regional models.* (London).

Runciman, W.G. 1966. *Relative deprivation and social justice.* (London).

Schneider, M. 1975. The quality of life in large American cities: objective and subjective social indicators. *Social indicators research,* 1, 495-509.

Singer, F. 1972. Our environment: control and costs. *The Conference Board Record,* quoted in U.S. Environmental Protection Agency (1973). *The quality of life concept.* (U.S. GPO, Washington D.C.).

Smith, D.M. 1973. *The geography of social well being in the United States.* (New York).

Smith, D.M. 1977. *Human geography: a welfare approach.* (London).

Stagner, R. 1970. Perceptions, aspirations, frustrations and satisfactions: an approach to urban indicators. *Annals of the American Academy of Political and Social Science,* 388, 59-68.

Stipak, B. 1977. Attitudes and belief systems concerning urban services. *Public Opinion Quarterly,* 41, 41-55.

Thorndike, E.L. 1939. *Your city.* (New York).

Thorndike, E.L. 1940. *144 smaller cities.* (New York).

Ward, Z.A. 1980. A policy antimony: public attitudes versus urban conditions in Western Europe, in Romanos, M.C. *Western European cities in crisis*. (Lexington Mass.).

Whitman, I. 1971. *Design of an environmental evaluation system*. (Columbus Ohio).

Wilson, J.O. 1967. *The quality of life in America*. (Mid West Research Institute, Kansas City).

Wingo, L. 1973. The quality of life: toward a microeconomic definition. *Urban Studies*, 10, 3-18.

Chapter 2

The Concept of Deprivation

George Gordon

INTRODUCTION

There is considerable historical evidence of spatial and social variations in the quality of life in Scotland. For example, the Victorian Reports of the Medical Officers of Health for Edinburgh (Littlejohn, 1865) and for Glasgow (Gairdner, 1870) revealed appalling spatial inequalities in living standards in that sharply dichoto-ised society. More recently the topic of social inequality has be-come the focus of renewed concern, investigation and policy initi-atives. Several overlapping, but differing, concepts related to the topic of social inequality have featured in this debate, namely: quality of life, social well-being, living standards, territorial and social justice, poverty and deprivation. The concepts of the quality of life, social well-being and living standards evaluate the whole spectrum. Whilst these can be measured by objective data, such as census indicators, many commentators believe that these con-cepts must incorporate an assessment of the individual's sense of well-being, of the critical factors affecting his or her quality of life. Knox and MacLaran (1978), in a study of 14 neighbourhood types in Dundee, found that weighting indicators of well-being by local values did not significantly affect the overall spatial pat-terns of quality of life in relation to health, housing, employment opportunities, personal security, income and consumption, leisure, social and political participation, access to amenities, environ-mental quality and social stability. Nonetheless the data on people's values indicated significant differences between the various types of area on nine criteria. Smith (1979), however, noted 'the extreme difficulty of establishing anything at all of substance about how groups of people differ with respect to their quality of life, subjectively perceived'. Smith doubted if it would be possible to devise a uniform areally comparable scale to measure and compare the sense of feeling about the quality of life by different people since that sense of feeling would inevitably be affected by their respec-tive life experiences.

Carley (1981) has described the growth of the social indicators movement in the 1960s, attributing the trend to the success and apparent limitations of economic indicators. The desire to develop measures of welfare and psychological satisfaction received con-siderable support from research councils and foundations. A flush of publications ensued including specialised journals such as Social Indicators Research. By the late 1970s the initial enthusiasm had dimmed as doubts were expressed about the feasibility of developing comparable measures of perceived quality of life, particularly since the concepts were frequently measured through surrogates, e.g. the concept of good health measured by life expectancy.

DEFINITION AND MEASUREMENT OF DEPRIVATION

The concepts of social justice, poverty and deprivation focus on particular parts of the spectrum, those experiencing an excess of 'bads' in terms of quality of life. Social justice (Runciman, 1972) explicitly embodies a remedial predisposition whereas the concepts of poverty and deprivation attempt to define a particular state. Poverty tends to generate images associated primarily with a state of income-deficiency but Abel-Smith and Townsend (1965) advocated a broader definition incorporating differences 'in home environment, material possessions and educational and occupational resources as well as financial resources'. The latter definition converges, conceptually and spatially, with deprivation. Berthoud (1976) defined deprivation as 'a lack of something other people have', whilst Holman (1978) suggested that it was 'a condition in which there is a failure to attain certain social norms to which existing social policies are apparently intended to provide access'. Deprivation has commonly been defined with reference either to agreed minimum standards or by high levels of deficiency on various criteria. It is not a single or simple concept. There are considerable practical and conceptual problems related to the measurement of deprivation which inevitably affect the precise meaning of the term. Deprivation is multi-dimensional and occurs in a variety of spatial settings.

Holtermann (1975) used 18 socio-economic indicators in her study of urban deprivation in Britain. In this context, indicators are meant to measure welfare, provide an insight into social and spatial inequalities and an input into corrective policy decision-making. Eleven indicators in the Holtermann study related to housing in terms of amenity, density and tenure. There were three economic indicators (male and female unemployment and percent unskilled manual workers), while the remaining variables measured car-ownership, life-cycle characteristics and immigrant status. She found particularly high levels of multiple deprivation in the conurbations, most notably Clydeside. For the detailed pattern 'on both single indicators and combinations of indicators it was found that ED's with extensive levels of deprivation generally occur within the conurbations, and that the local authorities making up the central cores of the conurbations contain proportionately more of them than the rest of the conurbation. Severe deprivation is found both in the inner areas dominated by private rental accommodation and on council estates, some in more peripheral locations' (Holtermann, 1975). Other studies by national government units (Scottish Office, 1980), local government (Liverpool Corporation, 1970) and academics (Smith, 1973) have incorporated non-Census variables relating to health, education and social problems in order to introduce further dimensions of the topic.

Geographers have concentrated upon a search for meaningful territorial social indicators of deprivation and well-being. Various spatial bases have been used although British studies have overwhelmingly favoured the enumeration district, the smallest available data unit. Whatever the spatial scale Census data for housing and employment are influenced by past and present local and regional policies. Hamnett (1979) cautioned against the fetishism of space. Some support for that view is provided by the Scottish Office study (1980) of Multiply Deprived Households in Scotland which found that, 'The deprived areas of Scotland which account for 11 per cent of all

Scottish households ... contain approximately 30 per cent of households with four or more deprivations'. Thus that the majority of
households with that level of deprivation did not live in the deprived areas. However 60 per cent of households with six or more
deprivations lived in deprived areas, apparently indicating a spatial concentration of severely deprived households. There is also
the problem of the relative importance of different dimensions of
deprivation and the comparative weighting of these dimensions and
these matters have generated a considerable technical debate.
    An influential study of multiple deprivation in Glasgow (Scottish
Development Department, 1973) suggested that almost one third of the
city consisted of areas of multiple deprivation. Subsequently
Strathclyde Regional Council (1976) proposed a scheme of fifty two
areas in Glasgow for Priority Treatment. These areas included districts of mixed and of local authority housing, in central and peripheral locations, and ranged in size from fewer than 700 to over
45 000 people. This diagnosis and treatment indicated that in
Glasgow ameliorative treatment was required in areas comparable in
population size to settlements such as Glenrothes.
    In fact, Strathclyde Region decided to implement initial action
in a regional total of forty five Areas of Priority Treatment although the 1981 policy review almost doubled that number. If the
magnitude of the task has been correctly identified it is doubtful
if much can be achieved in relation to several dimensions of deprivation without massive resource investment. Glasgow has benefited
from a considerable proportion of the Housing Corporation finances
in recent years which has been used in the rehabilitation and renewal of inner city districts. Monies from the Scottish Development
Agency and regional funds of the EEC have been used in much needed
environmental improvement schemes. Recently local authorities have
assumed a more active role in the field of the creation of employment through training schemes and the construction of advance fac-
tories. Finally the local authorities have invested in increased
educational and social work provision in deprived areas and in the
development of community participation and improvements in the quality and sensitivity of service provision.
    Deprivation is not an exclusively urban phenomenon but the gener-
ally high incidence rates in many urban settlements and the spatial
concentration of comparatively large numbers of multiply deprived
households in certain urban locations has inevitably attracted social
and political attention. In a study in the late 1960s of deprived
families Holman (1973) concluded that deprived areas were characterised by, 'inferior housing conditions, higher than average proportions of unskilled workers, persons in poverty, large families and
one-parent families; a lack of play and recreational facilities; a
high incidence of child deprivation and delinquency; and poorer
health than is found in the population as a whole.' Particular
social groups appear to have above average vulnerability to certain
forms of deprivation and recent research on the various syndromes
of deprivation (Coulter,1978) has been concerned with the spatial
associations of different kinds of deprivation.

Explanation of Deprivation

Despite the extensive literature on the topic of deprivation, Knox
(1982) notes that 'important conceptual and methodological issues
remain unresolved, not least of which is the question of defining
'deprivation' more rigorously'. Knox identified five theoretical
explanations of deprivation, namely: the culture of poverty; transmitted deprivation; institutional malfunctioning; maldistribution
of resources and opportunities; structural class conflict. Lawless
(1981) outlined how Government policy in Britain initially favoured
the culture of poverty and institutional malfunctioning themes whilst

17

subsequently many of the reports by the Community Development Project teams (Coventry 1975) indicated a structural class conflict interpretation. Lawless attached considerable importance to recent shifts in inner area policies towards an emphasis upon the generation of employment because he believed unemployment was the crucial component in severe deprivation.

The responses of local authorities can also be related to the various explanations of deprivation. Strathclyde Region in their deprivation strategy stressed five goals: positive discrimination; co-ordination with other levels of government and other agencies; altering staff attitudes and improving staff training; an overhaul of policies and practice; the development of community participation. There are obvious links to the theses of institutional malfunctioning and the maldistribution of resources in this strategy but the importance which was attached to the Born to Fail report (1973) indicated serious concern about transmitted deprivation. In that instance, positive discrimination in educational provision in deprived areas was the principal policy action. The inclusion of community participation sought local involvement as a safeguard against alienation and a state of hopelessness on the part of residents of deprived areas, the characteristic features of the culture of poverty thesis.

CONCLUSION

Doubtless significant progress can be achieved by improved administrative organisation and the engendering of more sympathetic attitudes and decision-making by managers and decision-takers in local and national government. It is, however, difficult to see how the overwhelming majority of multiple deprivation can be resolved without an extensive and powerful array of socio-economic policies related to employment, housing, health, social welfare and environmental conditions. Lawless (1981) believes that improved service delivery, whilst creating better access to certain resources and facilities, fails to tackle core facets of deprivation, notably unemployment. Government maintains a contrary view, believing that deprivation can be combatted by careful allocation and proper use of the resources at the disposal of local government. These differences of interpretation result in part from different political philosophies but also different diagnoses of the seriousness of the problem and of the desired minimal standard of improvement. If Lawless is correct about the critical role of unemployment in deprivation syndromes the current high levels of unemployment suggest that present policies will not resolve the problem of multiple deprivation because the fundamental economic and psychological components of deprivation do not feature prominently in local and regional policies and initiatives. Indeed it is possible that certain deprivations are increasing due to macro-economic factors and also to the development of new trends and problems. There is clearly a pressing need for independent monitoring of local and national government policies in relation to deprivation in order to evaluate success and to recognise lacunae and new areas of demand. Stipak (1977, 1979) has investigated the measurement of the performance of urban services and government agencies have implemented evaluative monitoring of various deprivation policies but there are considerable grounds for debate about the criteria adopted in the measurement of goal attainment. An associated issue concerns the realistic timescale for policies. Some government Urban Aid policies have been only partially successful because the timescale was too short. The decision of Strathclyde Region to increase the number of Areas of Priority Treatment illustrates the influence of mounting pressure

for action in other problem areas rather than the successful comple-
tion of the first phase of a policy. In fact action had only occurred in a fraction of the Areas of Priority Treatment designated at
the outset of the first phase of the regional deprivation strategy.
The re-evaluation of priorities inevitably involved changed perceptions of pressing needs and, in general, long term deprivation
strategies would also have to accommodate temporal changes in definitions of needs, problems, priorities and minimal standards and in
the spatial distribution of deprived households and the importance
of various syndromes.

Writing on housing Robson (1979) observed that 'even if, by
absolute standards, the very worst conditions were 'solved', a new
set of 'very worst' would automatically be created'. These remarks
are particularly apposite to deprivation studies which define 'worst'
by some arbitrary yardstick such as the bottom 5 per cent of enumeration districts on a particular dimension or composite indicator.
In absolute terms, that definition of deprivation is patently in-
soluble unless a cut-off is imposed of some acceptable minimal standard for that particular phenomenon.

The persistence of technical and conceptual problems in relation
to the definition and measurement of deprivation should not detract
from the recognition of the existence of a serious societal problem
or detract from the need for remedial action. Referring to social
indicators of conditions in Tower Hamlets in London, Smith (1979)
observed 'Indeed, they are hard to reconcile with the image of the
humane caring society supposedly fostered by Britain's Christian
tradition, liberal values and welfare state'. The search for more
penetrating definitions and more sensitive indicators and threshold
values, which is an essential task in the progressive search for
better policies, must not imply that economic and social hardships
are statistical, illusory, minor or transitory. Nevertheless effective policy demands incisive diagnosis and sound treatment. There
is a danger that politicians and funding bodies tire of an intractable problem and turn their attention to other targets. Often the
justification proffered is that the problem is now thoroughly understood and solutions are in hand. Our understanding of deprivation
and quality of life is certainly imperfect and much remains to be
done in terms of definition and measurement and in relation to the
development and monitoring of policies.

Politics impinge upon most areas of policy research and deprivation studies are no exception. The level of research funding and
the scale of budgets for remedial action are both ultimately influenced by politicians and their perceptions of priorities, their
political interpretations of societal priorities in expenditure at
the national and regional scale. In practice, the situation is constrained by legislation and by the limited avenues of political influence open to the public outside elections. Such topics are of
considerable relevance to the policy debate and are of interest to
political geographers and political scientists but they lie on the
periphery of the established geographical concern with territorial
social indicators and the development and evaluation of area based
policies.

REFERENCES

Abel-Smith, B. and Townsend, P. 1965. *The poor and the poorest*. (Bell, London).

Berthoud, R. 1976. *The disadvantages of inequality*. (MacDonald and Jane's, London).

Carley, M. 1981. *Social measurement and social indicators*. (George Allen and Unwin, London).

Coulter, J. 1978. *Grid-square census data as a source for the study of deprivation in British conurbations*. Working Paper 13, Census Research Unit, Department of Geography, University of Durham.

Coventry Community Development Project. 1975. *Final Report: Prosperity and the persistence of inequality*.

Gairdner, W.T. 1870. On defects of house construction in Glasgow as a cause of mortality. *Proceedings of the Philosophical Society of Glasgow*, vii, 245.

Hamnett, C. 1979. Area-based explanations: a critical appraisal. in *Social problems and the City*, Herbert D.T. and Smith, D. (eds), (Oxford University Press, Oxford), 244-260.

Holman, R. (ed) 1973. *Socially deprived families in Britain*. (Belford Square Press, London).

Holman, R. 1978. *Poverty*. (Martin Robertson, London).

Holtermann, S. 1975. Areas of urban deprivation in Great Britain. *Social Trends*, 6, 33-47.

Knox, P. 1982. *Urban Social Geography*. (Longman, London).

Knox, P. and MacLaran, A. 1978. Values and perceptions in descriptive approaches to urban-social geography, in *Geography and Urban Environment*, 1, Herbert, D.T. and Johnston, R.J. (eds), (Wiley, London), 197-247.

Lawless, P. 1981. *Britain's Inner Cities*. (Harper and Row, London).

Littlejohn, H. 1865. *Report on the sanitary conditions of the City of Edinburgh*. (Edinburgh).

Liverpool Corporation, 1970. *Social Malaise in Liverpool*. (Liverpool).

Robson, B. 1979. Housing, empiricism and the state, in *Social problems and The City*, Herbert, D.T. and Smith, D. (eds), 66-83.

Runciman, W.G. 1972. *Relative deprivation and social justice*. (Penguin, Harmondsworth).

Scottish Development Department, 1973. *Investigation to identify multiple deprivation areas*. Central Research Unit Paper No. 7.

Scottish Office, 1980. *A study of multiply deprived households in Scotland*. Central Research Unit Paper.

Smith, D.M. 1979. The identification of problems in cities: applications of social indicators, in *Social problems and The City*, Herbert, D.T. and Smith, D. (eds), 13-32.

Stipak, B. 1977. Attitude and belief systems concerning urban services. *Public Opinion Quarterly*, 41, 41-55.

Stipak, B. 1979. Are there sensible ways to analyse and use subjective indicators of urban service quality? *Social Indicators Research,* 6, 421-38.

Strathclyde Regional Council, 1976. *Urban deprivation.*

Wedge, P. and Prosser, H. 1973. *Born to fail.* National Children's Development Study. (National Children's Bureau).

Chapter 3

Poverty and Deprivation in the
West of Scotland

Michael Danson

INTRODUCTION

The common perception of British urban life in the early 1980s has come to be one of decaying inner cities and stagnating suburbs: any growth is reputedly restricted to free standing smaller towns and rural areas (Fothergill and Gudgin, 1982; Danson *et al.*, 1980). With the rediscovery of poverty in the 1960s in North America and Britain (see Gordon, 1972; Friedman, 1977), there have also arisen parallel paradigms on poverty and deprivation - one set founded on theories of segmentation in labour and product markets, the other on observations, dressed up as theories, of mismatches in labour and housing markets. The very desire of the Royal Scottish Geographical Society to convene a conference on this theme is evidence of the renewed and ongoing interest in the continuation and exist- ence of states of poverty within developed western society along a variety of dimensions.

What I shall try to do in this paper is firstly to briefly sum- marise the degrees and dimensions of poverty in the West of Scot- land. In a national context I shall claim that this area can just- ifiably be looked upon as having the most extensive poverty and de- privation in Britain. It is also frequently assumed or suggested that this environment is highly concentrated in, if not actually confined to, the inner city - we must also therefore consider whether Glasgow typifies the region or is in fact a degree worse - in effect whether it represents the nadir of British society. The comparative position of Northern Ireland, too often neglected in such analyses, remains untold here but the reader is referred to Evason (1980) and Child Poverty Action Group (1980) for some recent studies. In the second section I shall attempt to describe some of the causes and implications of the concentration and depth of poverty within the conurbation. Finally I intend to elaborate on the role of the present Government's policies and the recession in deepening these divides.

THE 'PROBLEM' STATED

Most people are aware of Holtermann's study (1975) of deprivation based upon the 1971 Census of Population: this showed Scotland, Clydeside in particular, with Glasgow at the focus, as having the greatest incidence of multiple deprivation in Britain, at the regional, conurbation and city level respectively. Overcrowding, lack of basic amenities, living at height, unemployment and so forth were all highly concentrated in this conurbation. Thus, for instance, almost one in five of Glasgow's population at that time lived in multiply deprived areas. During the 1970s we could probably add dampness, risk of hypothermia and generally high price levels to that list of social indicators where Clydeside appears to have Britain's poorest standards. The ownership of most consumer durables is likewise lower in the conurbation, suggesting that real incomes have been low over a long period of time. (Danson, 1979a,b) Further, as explained by others in the symposium, health and education are generally faltering in Scotland, with this area leading - if that is the correct word - the world in several aspects of twentieth century blight on the quality of life.

Several researchers have argued that there are in essence three forms of deprivation: housing, income and that arising from disability. As Holtermann's study suggests on the first of these forms, rural Scotland, urban Scotland outwith the conurbation, Clydeside and Glasgow are all much worse than expected when compared with the rest of Britain. However as we descend this urban system hierarchy within Scotland so the degree of relative deprivation increases with ultimately between 90 and 97 per cent of the very worst areas on Clydeside in Glasgow itself. Nevertheless along certain dimensions (deprivation) and along all dimensions (multiple deprivation) pockets of extreme poverty exist in nearly all the regions and towns of Britain. Table 3.1 demonstrates the overrepresentation of all parts of Scotland in the tally of both deprivation and multiple deprivation. Table 3.2 likewise confirms the position of Glasgow in the national and conurbation contexts.

When considering poverty arising from low incomes the sources of evidence are poor, particularly at the subregional level. However we can say that in Glasgow, the rest of Clydeside and elsewhere in Scotland real wages and salaries were lower than in comparable areas nationally. Although occupation by occupation the city and region frequently appear as having high wages - often second only to London and the South East of England - the job mix here is biased away from high paying sectors. As, if not more, important is the effect on money incomes of high prices north of the border - recent work by Danson (1979a,b,c) Scottish Consumer Council (1982) and Shah and Walker (1982) demonstrates that the neglect of this factor in looking at household incomes is severe. The 2-5 per cent money wage advantage enjoyed by male manual workers vis-a-vis the rest of Britain is more than negated by the 5-15 per cent higher charges for food, fuel, housing and transport and the greater need for expenditure on fuel and other goods - because of the climate, longer winter nights, isolation and peripherality. Together these two factors - higher prices and different expenditure patterns - suggest real wages of 90 per cent or less of the national average for each category of worker. Shah and Walker (1982) therefore find that their four constituent parts of Scotland occupy four of the lowest five positions as regards real income amongst British regions.

Within the conurbation, wages are undoubtedly lower for residents of the city than those of the suburbs and satellite towns on a job per job basis, with pay being more dependent on overtime, poorly policed wages councils' agreements, payments by results and so forth.

24

Table 3.1 Geographical distribution of Enumeration Districts
with multiple deprivation. Per cent in each Country,
Conurbation and Regional remainder: 1971

	All EDs in GB	Households over-crowded, male unemployment, lack excl. use of all base amenities (5% cut off level)	EDs exceeding 1% cut off value on 1 or more of 11 indicators.
Country:			
England	84.6	22.4	61.3
Wales	4.3	0.2	2.4
Scotland	11.1	77.4	36.3
Conurbation:			
London:inner	8.6	3.5	20.1
London:outer	10.4	0.2	3.4
Tyneside	2.0	1.3	4.3
W. Yorkshire	4.3	3.3	2.4
Merseyside	2.7	1.1	4.8
S.E. Lancashire	5.8	1.7	5.6
West Midlands	4.8	8.1	3.3
Clydeside	4.3	68.1	24.7
Region:			
Rest of South East	14.9	0.4	2.0
Rest of Northern	4.1	1.3	3.6
Rest of Yorks. & Humber	5.0	0.2	4.4
Rest of North West	5.4	-	2.2
Rest of West Midlands	4.2	0.6	0.7
East Midlands	5.0	0.6	2.0
East Anglia	2.0	-	0.4
South West	5.3	0.4	2.0
Rest of Scotland	6.8	9.4	11.7
	100.0	100.0	100.0

Source: Holtermann (1975)

25

Table 3.2   The worst 5% of the Clydeside Conurbation's
             Enumeration Districts on individual indicators -
             proportion in Glasgow 1971

INDICATOR

Overcrowded households (>1.5 persons per room)	97%
Lack exclusive use of all basic amenities	94%
Males unemployed, but seeking work or sick	90%
Percentage of EDs in Glasgow	55%

Source: Holtermann (1975)

One of the primary sources of income, however, for all areas
within Britain, and indeed for many households the only source, is
state benefit. A key indicator of this dependence is given by the
activity rate amongst those of working age: in 1981 Strathclyde's
figure for males, at 89.9 per cent was nationally low, with Glasgow
the lowest in the region (89.1 per cent). By contrast, the female
(single, widowed, divorced) rate for the city (73.9 per cent) was
high in Strathclyde (71.4 per cent), similarly the married women's
rate (56.8 per cent) was the highest outwith the New Towns. Together these results suggest that many families in Strathclyde, and
Glasgow especially, lack any earned income, whilst many more are
forced to rely on a second wage to be kept out of poverty, with
service jobs also being more available in the core city. To encap-
sulate these statistics in one figure and to demonstrate the degree
of reliance on state benefits we can compare the proportion of the
population in full-time work across areas, i.e. the 'dependency
ratio'. Nationally this is 34.4 per cent, in Scotland it is lower
at 33.9 per cent, in the conurbation lower still at 33.2 per cent
and in Glasgow, at 31.4 per cent, extremely low: implying that each
worker must support almost 10 per cent extra people than in Britain
as a whole.
    Unemployment, naturally, is the clearest indicator of poverty
and one of its major causes - both at the time of joblessness and
through the life cycle, reducing the eventual pension to the basic
minimum. In early 1982 the male unemployment rate in Glasgow stood
at 24 per cent, with rates over 30 per cent in the north and east
of the city where a quarter of a million people lived. Indeed the
six highest rates, at Employment Exchange level, in Strathclyde
region were all within Glasgow. Youth unemployment was over 59 per
cent at that time in the region with the city again registering one
of the highest rates. In the eastern end of the conurbation, in
Monklands and Motherwell, male unemployment was over 25 per cent
and rising, with similar figures in the old industrial areas
of Clydebank, Kilmarnock and Greenock, being especially high in
the mining areas of Lanarkshire and Ayrshire. Compounding the problems of unemployment are the high proportions suffering from re-
peated and lengthy spells of idleness: each of which not only de-
moralises but also feeds local depression (economic, social and
political) by depriving workers of their rights to national insurance benefits and forcing them onto means-tested benefits. With
approximately one in four households across the country being
pensioner-only and with the vast majority of these in our areas
being dependent, effectively, solely on the state old-age pension
(for the reasons given in the two paragraphs above), about 25 per

cent of all households in Glasgow and Clydeside are on the poverty
line on this criterion alone. To these should be added the numbers
on unemployment, sickness, supplementary and similar benefits. (By
definition the Supplementary Benefit level represents the officially
determined poverty line, however as this excludes housing costs and
in recent years has not been fully indexed, a figure of 140 per
cent of this rate is usually taken. From Pond (1981), various definitions coincidentally suggest that an income of £74-£75 per week
would have represented 'the poverty line' in the financial year
1980-81.) In 1981, then, preliminary tabulations from the Census of
Population suggest that roughly 37-40 per cent of households were
living at or below the poverty line in Glasgow and slightly less in
the region as a whole.

Other sources of income (self employment, capital investments
and state benefits), all show evidence of reinforcing the relative
income poverty described above. Self employment is very low in
Scotland generally, consequent as it is, to a large extent, on the
level of real personal disposable income in the community. Poverty
wages and benefits leave little room for small business formation
and expansion into the consumer and service markets. A buoyant
local economy is thus crucial for the generation of such opportunities; similarly there are close interrelationships between local
prosperity and profits and the ownership of capital - investments,
stocks and shares. So although Edinburgh can justifiably claim to
be one of the world's leading financial and investment centres, the
general populous of Scotland and the deprived urban west in particular have little income from capital sources. This irony of extreme
plenty amongst massive poverty is unfortunately too often lost to
commentator and public alike, and all the more poignant given the
existence of North Sea Oil. It is possible therefore to discern
circles of virtue within the prosperous capital of the UK and its
hinterland juxtaposed with vicious circles in the North and West and
in the inner cities of the nation.

In income terms, then, using the few available data sources for
the city and region, it is obvious that poverty arising from dependence on state benefits or low pay is a major and widespread problem.
If we consider some of the factors that underpin this aspect of
poverty - large family size, single parent families, lack of a
second income and, of course, unemployment - then we see Glasgow,
the conurbation and to a lesser extent the rest of Scotland badly
placed on each indicator. Again the position of the former of these
is expressed by the 'Demographic Indicators' published by Strathclyde Regional Council (1981). Using five key statistics measured
at postcode level to identify relative poverty within the region
this suggests that of the worst 30 areas in Strathclyde, 25 are in
Glasgow and half of the population of the city live in neighbourhoods of extreme multiple deprivation. Of note, Glasgow has high
concentrations of young mothers, manual workers and illegitimate
children - all strongly associated with poverty and deprivation
amongst the young and subsequently through their lives. Outwith the
core city, and closely correlated with high male unemployment, child
poverty is concentrated within each district's 'dump estate' and,
though not so extensively, in the old declining industrial areas of
Motherwell, Airdrie/Coatbridge, Greenock and Kilmarnock. So deprivation as measured by housing problems is reinforced by deprivation
from income and need related factors. Again although the data is
poor, the proportion of families suffering low living standards
because of disability is once more higher in Glasgow with a census
proxy, 'permanently sick', being six times greater (at 3.3 per cent
of non pensioner adults) than in more prosperous areas.

To summarise: in housing, income and disability terms, deprivation is particularly widespread on Clydeside, especially in the old, inner industrial core and, though it is by no means an urban or conurbation problem, the concentration here cannot be overstated. So whereas London, Merseyside and Tyneside amongst other localities have instances and intensities of each of these indicators and forms of poverty, and have certain areas - the inner city in particular - of multiple deprivation, I believe it is only on Clydeside with Glasgow at the focus that deprivation reaches such levels on such a scale.

EXPLANATIONS AND IMPLICATIONS

We have, then, described the parameters of the standards of living in the West of Scotland, now we must attempt to explain the origins of the poverty and deprivation revealed and the causes of this apparent spatial inequality.

From several studies we can now state with some certainty that the principal causes of poverty are low pay, unemployment and old age. These three interact with each other and also, crucially for some groups, with sickness and disability. For the majority of the poor, wherever they live in Great Britain, the origins of their own poverty are primarily to be found in low pay and unemployment during their working lives. Further, since the mid 60s employment decline has been biased towards male, skilled, manual and manufacturing jobs - all of which have been lost at faster rates in the inner cities and by inner city residents.

Conversely growth has taken place in female, semiskilled, and junior non-manual service jobs. Spatially there has generally been a drift of jobs away from traditional industrial areas and towards new and small free-standing towns. In Clydeside as a whole within manufacturing there has been deskilling of the workforce, a trend that has continued for over half a century. To quote Payne (1977): 'Clearly, Scotland has become more working class and its population is less skilled vis-a-vis England than at any time since the First World War'. Complementary analyses could be undertaken for the other 'Assisted Areas' in Britain.

Underpinning these developments have been parallel and interacting geographical and industrial processes. Output, at national and international levels, has become more and more concentrated within larger and larger multiregional and multinational corporations, whilst, simultaneously, higher functions have been centralized for both these firms and Government administrations progressively up the urban hierarchy. With the production process itself being fragmented - invention, innovation, prototype development and R & D generally drawn to the centre, mass production and assembly forced out to the periphery with a footloose status - the conurbations have suffered as the dynamics of these tendencies logically worked themselves out spatially. Thus both traditional jobs, located in integrated plants, and local control were continuously lost by the inner cities.

A series of shift-share analyses on the Clydeside economy for the period 1841-1977 demonstrated a long period of job losses from the inner city - in line with the performances of the other British conurbations - with the outer suburbs and industrial towns following this pattern of decline after the mid 60s (Danson, 1980). These results cannot be explained by the industrial structure of Glasgow or its equivalent in the other conurbations; rather it is primarily the outcome of a failure to grow in the services and public sector - especially in health and education - at the same rate as the rest of Britain. This was a general big city phenomenon: the movement out of population produced a concomitant movement out or non-uniform growth of jobs - basically expansion was demand led. The non-replacement of traditional jobs in the core cities was a national problem by contrast; employment declines in steel, shipbuilding, coal, textiles and so forth represented losses to Britain as a whole, with increasing capital intensities leading to new plants in these and other industries to seek greenfield sites.

From the activity rates discussed earlier we know that males in the inner city have less opportunity to work so that relatively more drop out of the labour force or are forced to quit because of health problems, associated with poverty itself. It was also noted that married women have a greater need to and opportunity to seek work, this mainly being in the low paying, unskilled sectors of clothing, food, drink and tobacco, services, etc., all of which are still clustered around the city centres of the conurbations to make use of agglomeration economies. Thus the wage rates in these industries are bid down by the large, underemployed labour force and are only maintained at these levels by the Wages Councils' agreements. The inner city labour market is therefore typically 'competitive' in neoclassical economics terminology, founded on high horizontal worker mobility, cyclical sensitivity and low training (formal and informal), (Danson, 1982).

In the relatively isolated outer conurbation localities and beyond them in rural and semi-rural areas, employers are faced with slightly different labour market conditions. Often divorced from traditionally strong unionized workforces there is a tendency for wages to be suppressed, though not to the same extent as in the homogenous labour market of the inner city. Obviously the results of the processes of change described are exaggerated but the tendencies towards dichotomy were much in evidence up to the mid 70s. Thereafter, in an outward flowing wave, the inner city problem overtook the older industrial outer conurbation, and, in the present recession, to many of the erstwhile successful free-standing towns. Further, with ongoing technological advances and associated restructuring of national and international economies the continuing redivision of labour will mean that in low skilled, assembly work and the like, British labour - and conurbation workers in particular - will be competing with the Newly Industrializing Developing Countries: wages again being bid down.

So, overall, there are strong forces depressing real wages of many sections of the working class in the developed world, with the inner cities, though also increasingly the outer conurbations, suffering most. Small firms and plants, as well as certain industrial sectors, are concentrated in the inner city, and as they bring flexibility to the whole economic system - through subcontracting and high birth/death rates - so they engender instability in the labour force. All these factors, to reiterate, are disproportionately felt in the centre city and indeed show that for the economic system to maintain its existence, uneven development must take place. The inner city problem is therefore describing the spatial outcome of these processes. As regards city residents' quality of life, poverty at work is reproduced as poverty in sickness (with benefit tied to wage income), poverty in youth (with a lack of apprenticeships and other stable employment opportunities) and poverty in old age (with less ability to enter superannuation schemes and acquire national insurance contributions).

TENDENCIES AND TRIBULATIONS

From the mid 70s the decline of the inner cities, or more correctly of their residents, was to accelerate before a period of precipitous fall in living standards was introduced by the new Conservative Government. Not only did the recession deepen markedly during these years but also the new administration moved dramatically away from the Butskellite tradition of previous post war governments. There was in consequence a fundamental change in the proportion of the poor who were unemployed, low paid, sick and in large or single parent families; the old and the disabled declined relatively though their numbers and the depth of their poverty both increased markedly.

Elected on a Manifesto that promised to restore incentives and increase personal freedom, the Conservative Government quickly embarked on a set of policies that not only accelerated growing inequality and falling living standards for the poor, but also radically changed and undermined the Welfare System itself. (See Danson, 1983 for background).

Given the move against families with children in the last 25 years, the failure to increase Child Benefit in 1979 was particularly disappointing. Increases in later budgets were at less than the rate of inflation so that by the end of 1981 the net cut in support to children was 5.7 per cent. To the recipients of national insurance benefits, the additions for children were repeatedly cut, so that there were high falls in the level of support given to the children of the poorest families. The only exceptions to this were one-parent families who in this repect were protected from inflation.

For unemployment and sickness benefit claimants, there were several decreases in income: despite many being below the tax threshold, these benefits were increased at five per cent less than inflation, in lieu of taxation, in 1980, and by one per cent less than inflation in 1980, and by two per cent in 1981. There was thus a cumulative fall in these of at least eight per cent to the end of 1981, with numerous technical adverse changes also. More important even than this, the major reason for national insurance benefits maintaining their position up to 1971, Earnings Related supplements, was abolished on January 3rd 1982. At one stroke the incomes of the short term unemployed and sick were cut by another 12.5 per cent on average.

The link between national insurance benefits' increases and price/average earnings increases (whichever was higher) was broken in 1979, in future only price inflation was to be matched. This would have cost pensioners ten per cent in the late 70s if in force then. Welfare State recipients were thus not to share in national prosperity - rising real incomes.

The uprating date of benefits was pushed back a fortnight and Exceptional Needs Payments - only the poorest being eligible - were replaced with more restrictive Single Payments and Urgent Needs Payments. These alterations continued the previous undermining of the poor's position though the philosphy behind this had changed.

All Welfare claimants lost in real and relative terms post 1979, but their stigmatisation has also increased. Although estimates of tax evasion and fraud were regularly and reliably between 100 and 1000 times greater than Social Security fraud, the new Government cut the inspectors investigating the former, increased those in the latter and decreased those officials 'advising' clients. Similarly wage inspectors were reduced. There were therefore consistent changes in emphasis, with little or no evidence that these were related to efficiency criteria.

Turning to the tax burden, the Government made several important steps. By failing to increase tax thresholds, abolishing the lower rates or bands, and decreasing the higher rates, there was a massive shift of the tax burden onto those with less than average earnings and a concomitant increase in the poverty trap. (The poverty trap is caused by the overlap between eligibility for means-tested benefits and liability for income tax and national insurance contributions). Government changes 1979-81 in housing policy alone increased the numbers of taxpayers in the poverty trap in the UK from at least 1.5 million to at least 2.5 million. In net terms it meant that 98 per cent of taxpayers were on a single marginal rate, making the UK system the least progressive in the world. As said above, as tax reliefs are not cash limited, this position was not incompatible with the rest of the Government's strategy.

Increases in National Insurance contributions, already regressive in 1979, have hit the poor low paid particularly hard. Coupled with the tax changes, there is now a hollow at 1.75 - 2.25 average earnings where the marginal tax rate falls to 30 per cent from 38.75 per cent. Exchequer contributions to the NI Fund have continued to fall, down to 14 per cent from 18 per cent in 1980. Thus a lower proportion has come from general taxation, which is still slightly progressive, and a higher proportion from national insurance contributions - regressive, so overall the NI Fund has become more regressively funded. It has also returned surpluses for several years, a staggering actuarial outcome given the present needs of the insured population.

Doubling VAT overnight for non-luxury, non-necessary goods, increasing excise duties and taxes on Giffen goods, and shifting the burden of Local Authority income onto rates - from progressive general taxation - all tended to make expenditure taxation and indirect taxation in the main even more regressive.

Thus the Conservative Government's taxation policy was to make income taxes proportional - rather than progressive, and indirect taxation more regressive. Also there were shifts from direct onto indirect, unearned income onto earned, companies onto individuals: in net terms from the rich onto the poor, from those who own for a living onto those who work or make themselves available for work.

Not only did the Government fail in its commitment to increase incentives to work - it increased the depth and breadth of the poverty trap, it also increased the overall tax burden of the UK population. As a proportion of GNP, income taxes and social security contributions increased by 2.3 per cent 1979-80, apart from Eire, the highest increases in OECD. This proportion was higher in mid 1981 than when Labour left office in 1979. By late 1981 it was higher than at any time in our history, and in 1982 it passed 45.7 per cent of GNP. Remember this tax burden has also shifted since 1979 heavily against the lower income groups. Capital taxation, of course, has decreased in real, relative and absolute terms.

The final consideration of the Government's record concerns their general policies on prices, subsidies, charges and wages. Decreased support for Local Authorities, Nationalized Industries, educational establishments and so forth have increased prices, charges and rates in these sectors by degrees greater than the average for inflation. Forming as they do a greater part of the poor's budgets, being mainly basic goods and services, the linking of the increase in benefits to the general RP1 inevitably underestimates the fall in the living standards of the poor.

Manual pay in the public sector has increased more slowly than non-manual - as indeed it has in the private sector, so even where the Government has direct control over poverty, many manual workers earn less than the Family Income Supplement levels - they did not seek to change this through wage policy. Again increased charges for NHS, school meals and milk and so on have all disproportionately affected the lower income groups. The position of women has been especially badly affected with reduced child care, nursery and abortion facilities forcing women to stay at home; redundancies in Education, Local Authorities and the NHS also hitting women harder. Moreover, in the International Year of the Disabled Person, the Government ended the Disabled Quotas scheme. So there were profound, fundamental and, for some, irreversible changes post 1979. Overall the Government has spent more on Defence and Law and Order, less on social programmes.

CONCLUSION

Glasgow, with greater numbers already in the groups most at risk from suffering a low standard of living, has thus experienced both a deepening and a widening of poverty and deprivation over the last few years as a result of deindustrialisation and the above changes in social policy. Beyond the city, and in the old industrial towns especially, similar regression has occurred. Reinforcing future tendencies towards a continuation of this loss are the very programmes aimed at regeneration: the attention given to small firms, the provision of enterprise zones, the diminution of the laws and rights of protection given to the low paid, women and the sick, the cuts in public expenditure, and creeping privatisation - all have created the conditions for further cuts in the quality of life of the poor. The circles of virtue and vice described previously have been accentuated: each change in taxation, benefits, charges, expenditure and law has led to a further bifurcation of British society. Popularly seen as a North-South dichotomy, these cumulative developments in effect have isolated the poor - materially, socially and spiritually - from the rest of the population, whilst contradictly underlining the threat of poverty that the vast majority face through redundancy, disability, old age, etc.

Therefore, in conclusion, it can be strongly argued that the 'inner city problem' is (just as the regional problem was and is) founded on low pay and unemployment, and thus on the spatial outcome of underlying economic and social processes. Policies to reduce low pay and unemployment are a prerequisite for dealing with geographical inequality, though not sufficient on their own. Present actions (early 1983) are exacerbating poverty and deprivation in the West of Scotland, neither are they creating the conditions for the removal of these blights.

REFERENCES

Child Poverty Action Group, 1980. *Northern Ireland: Depriving the Deprived*. Poverty, No. 8 (CPAG, London).

Danson, M.W. 1979a. Relative Real Incomes in Scotland. *Scottish Trade Union Review*, 5, 19-20.

Danson, M.W. 1979b. Low pay and the poverty line. *Scottish Trade Union Review*, 6, 29-32.

Danson, M.W. 1979c. Prices and poverty in rural Scotland. *Scottish Trade Union Review*, 7, 29-32.

Danson, M.W. 1982. The industrial structure & labour market segmentation: Urban & regional implications. *Regional Studies*, 16(4), 255-265.

Danson, M.W. 1983. *The decline & fall of the Welfare State.* (University of Glasgow, Dept. of Social & Economic Research, Mimeo, Glasgow).

Danson, M.W., Lever, W.F. and Malcolm, J.F. 1980. The Inner City employment problem in Great Britain, 1952-76: A shift-share approach. *Urban Studies,* 17, 193-210.

Evason, E. 1980. *Poverty in Belfast,* Child Poverty Action Group, Research Series, No. 8 (London).

Fothergill S, and Gudgin, G. 1982. *Unequal growth: urban and regional employment change in the UK.* (Heinnemann Educational Books, London).

Friedman, A.L. 1977. *Industry & labour: class struggle at work and monopoly capitalism.* (Macmillan, London).

Gordon, D.M. 1972. *Theories of poverty and underemployment.* Lexington, (D.C. Heath, Lexington, Mass.).

Holtermann, S. 1975. Areas of urban deprivation in Great Britain: an analysis of 1971 Census data. *Social Trends,* 6.

Mackay, G.A. and Laing, G. *Consumer problems in rural areas.* (Scottish Consumer Council, Glasgow).

Pond, C, 1981. *Low pay - 1980's style.* Low Pay Review, No. 4, (Low Pay Unit, London).

Shah, A. and Walker, M. 1982. *The distribution of regional earnings in the UK.* (University of Newcastle, Department of Economics, Mimeo, Newcastle).

Strathclyde Regional Council, 1981. *Demographic indicators 1976-78: An analysis of vital statistics by post code.* (Strathclyde Regional Council, Chief Executive's Department, Glasgow).

Chapter 4

Strathclyde's Strategy to

Combat Deprivation

Keith Yates

INTRODUCTION

The first Regional Council elections in May 1974 saw the establishment of the Council prior to taking over its responsibilities in
May 1975. During this period the Council recognised the prime importance in tackling the problems of deprivation across Strathclyde.
In this respect a number of key events can be traced which highlighted the need for such a commitment. The National Children's
Bureau report *'Born to Fail?'* (Wedge and Prosser, 1973) showed that
the incidence of poor housing, low wages or unemployment and family
circumstances combined to prevent many children obtaining equal
opportunities. Moreover, it showed that whilst only one in 14 children suffered from a combination of these factors in the United
Kingdom, in Strathclyde one in six children were Born to Fail? The
Department of Environment carried out a systematic analysis of the
1971 Census (Holtermann,1975) which showed conclusively that, whichever 'indicators of deprivation' were selected, Clydeside topped
the national league in the scale and intensity of deprivation.
These two studies were important in that they focussed national
attention on the problems in Strathclyde and helped to engender a
climate for establishing a strategy to combat deprivation. Equally
important from the point of view of defining the strategy were a
series of studies or experiences taking place within the region.
Thus, the *West Central Scotland Plan,* published in 1974, provided a
strategy not only for land use development but also for social and
economic development in the region. Its proposals were very germane
to the Council's emerging deprivation policy. For the first time
social objectives were built into development and redevelopment proposals. The plan argued that many regional policy measures in the
1960s had failed, despite good intentions, to tackle the local problems of unemployment and deprivation. In short, conditions in the
region were very polarised and macro regional policies had exacerbated these differences. At the same time a number of important
experiments were beginning to emerge, each with similar objectives
to improve local communities through the joint involvement of departments and the community. In Glasgow environmental improvement
was the spur, in Greenock/Port Glasgow, social work, in Paisley, the
Government sponsored Community Development Project (CDP) and in
Motherwell, local corporate planning.

THE DEPRIVATION STRATEGY

The establishment of the Regional Council fused together many of the
lessons of these various developments and the momentum for change
created by the national attention was harnessed to formulate the
Council's deprivation strategy.

When the Council put forward its regional strategy in its
'Regional Report' in 1976 Strathclyde Regional Council, (SRC, 1976)
it stated that the two key factors were: a) the need to increase
the number of jobs in the region b) the need to tackle urban deprivation. The Council advanced its proposals to tackle deprivation
in a further document *'Multiple Deprivation'* (the Red Book) which
was approved by the Council in October, 1976. The policy rested
upon a recognition that the main components required in a serious
attempt to tackle deprivation should be:

    i)   a policy of positive discrimination
    ii)   a comprehensive review of existing policies and practice
    iii) staff training and changing traditional attitudes
    iv)   co-ordination between Central/Local Government and other
          agencies such as the Health Boards, and
    v)   community participation

Whilst this policy was based upon the Council's own analysis of
the problems, it was not dissimilar to the Government's policy for
inner cities announced a year later in the *Inner City White Paper*
of 1977. The 1971 Census showed that market forces and public
policies had created gross spatial inequalities in Strathclyde.
More than any other conurbation in Britain, the social and economic
conditions in Strathclyde were highly polarised. These conditions
have persisted since 1975 as has been shown by the Demographic Indicators of Deprivation (SRC, 1982) and various independent research
studies. Male unemployment rates are over 30 per cent in many Areas
for Priority Treatment (APTs), over ten per cent of households are
headed by single parents and 15 per cent of births are illegitimate.
Social work studies have shown that 70 per cent of children coming
into care come from families whose head is unemployed or a single
parent, 60 per cent come from the APTs. More disturbingly, children
in care from APTs are less likely to be fostered, by a factor of
five. All this evidence clearly indicates that the inequalities
persist and that policies are required to redress the life chances
of those suffering from deprivation.

Areas for Priority Treatment

The analysis in the Regional Report had identified 114 areas of
multiple deprivation within Strathclyde (SRC, 1976b). These areas
contained 30 per cent of the region's population. A corporate group
of officers examined services in those areas and selected a smaller
number (45) of APTs. In adopting an area based strategy for tackling deprivation, the Council accepted an approach, which whilst
recognising economic inequalities and family circumstances led to
deprivation, also believed that there was a gross maldistribution of
resources - local government and other agencies were augmenting disadvantage by their practice and policies. The Council's strategy
recognises the main causes of deprivaton as:

    i)   the national economic circumstances and the relative
          poverty of those dependent upon state benefits
    ii)   the operation of the housing market and of social
          services, which often tend to reinforce the problems

iii)   certain managerial deficiencies of government and, in
       some instances, the attitudes and practices of depart-
       ments which were either insensitive or unsympathetic to
       the needs of the disadvantaged
iv)   the apathy and sense of hopelessness that exists in many
       communities as a result of years of neglect.

The strategy was primarily area based because it was recognised
that problems were highly concentrated and services were usually
delivered through localised service outlets - the school, community
centre, bus services, social work offices. However, an important
part of the strategy has also been the thematic or client based
approach, either by member/officer working groups or through the
development of services for disadvantaged groups such as the homeless or handicapped who are not so concentrated in areas of deprivation as other groups such as the single parent, the unemployed
and families at risk. Thus whilst there is a logic and administrative neatness about an area based policy, it is only a part of the
total strategy and the Council has always sought to tackle deprivation wherever it exists through more sensitive service delivery.
     The Council's strategy was initially to be one of 'putting our
own house in order', and certainly differed from the traditional
West of Scotland response which was to request or urge more resources
to be made available. The Red Book was clear that deprivation could
only be tackled effectively by a co-ordinated response of members
and officers from Central and Local Government closely involved with
the community in a two way educative, regenerative process. To have
any significant impact the policy would require certain additional
initiatives. These were:

i)   bringing pressure on the Central Government and all other
      relevant agencies to deal with the problems of poverty
ii)   promoting concerted action to bring about economic re-
      generation of multiply deprived areas
iii) encouraging housing authorities to alter their policies
      with a view to alleviating the housing problems of de-
      prived areas and attempting to achieve a more balanced
      population mix in these areas
iv)   ensuring that the public services in deprived areas are
      relevant to the needs of the area, adequate in scale,
      readily accessible, well co-ordinated and sensibly
      administered and
v)   recognising that the reactivation of community spirit
      in these areas has a major role to play in their regener-
      ation.

IMPLEMENTATION AND REVIEW

The five years that have elapsed since the adoption of the strategy
contained in the Red Book have seen considerable progress towards
implementing many aspects of the deprivation policy.

Positive discrimination and improved service delivery

Although the APTs were largely areas with a preponderance of public
sector housing and services, they did not in 1975 receive favourable
public services compared to other parts of the region. Moreover,
the absence of private sector provision in the APTs exacerbated the
often poor public sector provision. Because the income level of
households in APTs is insufficient to support a wide variety of
activities normally provided by the private sector, the provision
of good and relevant public sector services is of utmost importance.

When the Council examined services in the APTs, they were generally
found to be worse than average. Schools were poorly staffed owing
to the shortage of teachers and the reluctance of staff to serve
for long in schools with large classes and poor reputations. The
same predicament was found in social work; the most difficult areas
had great difficulty recruiting and keeping staff. A survey of
public transport in APTs showed that the unreliability and high cost
of transport were the problems most often cited by residents.
Numerous community surveys have also shown that the condition of
roads, pavements and lighting left a great deal to be desired.
Outside the region's responsibility, although equally important,
housing problems included a poor environment, overcrowding and the
general low reputation of the areas through years of misguided
allocation policies. Health services in APTs also appear to be less
than adequate bearing in mind that the level of health provision in
Strathclyde as a whole compares well with other parts of Britain.
Various health indices point towards a poor level of general health
in Strathclyde. Perinatal mortality and life expectancy are both
considerably worse than average. Again this conceals even more disturbing trends in the APTs. Thus the infant death rate in Easterhouse is 22.0 per 1000 live births compared with 8.7 in Bearsden
and Milngavie. This correlates to the proportion of manual workers
and confirms the national evidence of the DHSS report on
'Inequalities in Health' (Black, 1982). Recent research has also
shown the disturbing effect of increasing unemployment on health.
     The region has used the first five years constructively in
making a start. Positive discrimination is probably a misnomer;
what has happened is that the region has achieved a levelling up of
some services in the deprived areas. In the context of a period of
declining resources it has been made difficult, other than by use
of the Urban Programme, to actually move towards full positive discrimination. The Education Department has moved, since reorganisation, towards providing comparable or better staffing in the APTs,
than other areas. The effect of declining rolls and the ability
to recruit and deploy staff across the whole region have helped the
Education Department to eliminate part-time education and achieve
national standards in staffing in the APTs. In addition the extra
staffing provided through either Circular 991 or the Urban Programme
have been almost entirely deployed in areas of need ensuring a
slightly better pupil/teacher ratio in APT schools. Other progress
has been made largely through use of the Urban Programme - thus new
nursery schools and classes, home/school link teachers, extra
careers staff and the development of community centres have all been
largely dependent upon the Urban Programme. The development of
community education services, particularly in the field of adult
basic education, has been considerable and largely funded through
mainline resource provision. The Social Work Department has also
been able, in a period when the basic grade establishment has increased from 289 to 712, to divert staff to the APTs. Again they
often started well behind but as the Social Work Needs and Resources
studies have shown the APT areas now have a better level of staffing
per head of population than other areas - not that this is totally
adequate as the scale of problems is dependent on factors other than
the total population. Unlike Education, Social Work has been growing
during the five years since the strategy was introduced and in
several areas it has been possible to develop new services in line
with the deprivation stategy. Community work and welfare rights
have expanded almost ten fold and the majority of the new staff have
been deployed in the APT areas. Other developments mainly funded
through the Urban Programme, include children and family centres,
social groupworkers, family aides, day carers, homemakers and a
number of projects aimed at special client groups such as the single
homeless, battered wives and alcoholics. Voluntary organisations

have provided many of these services and many have co-operated fully
in the implementation of the strategy. Whilst there is not time in
a paper of this length to highlight progress by all departments it
is worthwhile to note the community projects carried out by the
police in the APT areas, the special shopper buses and workers'
services provided to peripheral housing schemes in Glasgow by the
PTE, and the road and lighting improvements carried out by the Roads
Department. However, there probably has been a tendency to pursue
deprivation policies through the personal services of Education and
Social Work, and even in these services there remains scope for
positive discrimination in mainline provision. Whilst these developments will be significant, there is an equally important need for
positive discrimination to be pursued by infrastructure and resource
departments.

Outside the activities of the Council, the greatest progress
has been made in housing. Through the Housing Plan system the
Council has participated with the 19 District Council's in Strathclyde in establishing housing need, reviewing allocation policies
and assessing priorities. Eligibility for local authority housing
has much improved - and in some Districts a real attempt has been
made to avoid allocation policies which concentrate 'at risk' and
problem families in certain schemes. Unfit housing and inconsider-
ate allocation policies are closely linked with poor educational
performance and deteriorating social conditions: the one reinforces
and perpetuates the effects of the other. The massive switch of
emphasis to special need housing (sheltered housing, single person
housing and large family housing) and modernisation rather than new
build is consistent with the Council's deprivation strategy but has
been negated by the halving of the housing capital allocations in
recent years (although allocation practice still discriminates
against single people, single parent families and other young
families). There are already several examples of a combination of
reduced housing investment and continued allocation practices
causing whole areas to deteriorate beyond repair. When this occurs
in areas where the Council has made a genuine commitment of resources
and has encouraged a wide variety of community activities, then the
policy is patently absurd and must be arrested. These reductions
are also affecting to a lesser extent the housing associations who
were poised to make big inroads into the legacy of run down tenemental property in the Region. Some joint progress with District
Councils has continued with the provision of group tenancies for the
handicapped and homeless.

In developing policies of positive discrimination and seeking
to improve service delivery the Council undertook to form a partner-
ship with the SDA, SSHA and Glasgow District Council in the GEAR
project and to introduce experimental area co-ordination schemes
with District Councils in seven areas of the Region.

The Glasgow Eastern Area Renewal Project (GEAR)

The Glasgow Eastern Area Renewal project was set up by the Secretary
of State in 1976 and was the forerunner of inner city partnerships
which are now developing in England. The Council has given the area
high priority in improving services and carrying out redevelopment.
A co-ordinator was appointed in April 1977 and the area has benefited considerably through Urban Programme projects, as well as
mainline programmes. Although the problems of GEAR remain extensive,
it is only one of Strathclyde's APTs and in recent years the Council
has recognised that greater emphasis should be directed towards the
other APTs which benefited only marginally in the early years of
the Council's strategy.

Area Initiatives

Seven area initiatives each headed by a seconded area co-ordinator
linking to Region and District Councils began operation in 1978 and
have provided a useful means to implement the deprivation policy as
well as a learning exercise. In a positive way they have accelerated community development, released the energy of many capable
fieldwork staff and have been at the forefront of positive discrimination policies, particularly through the Urban Programme.
  One initiative, the Doon Valley, terminated in 1980 and another
Greenend/Sykeside in Coatbridge in 1981. Two further initiatives
have since been established. Whilst the initiatives provide a realistic and practical way of getting things going in an area, they are
no substitute for the long term changes that are required across the
whole region. It is particularly noted that most progressive developments in initiative areas have been funded through the Urban
Programme. The initiatives were intended to challenge the traditional methods of service delivery and in this sense they have confirmed the inertness of departments to respond to new methods of
working. The onus is now on the Council to utilise the experience
of the initiatives to foster innovative practice and provide more
relevant mainline services.

Urban Programme

An important element in positive discrimination policies has been
the Government's Urban Programme which now provides £15m in current
expenditure and £5m of new capital expenditure each year. Whilst
there is no longer real growth in the Urban Programme, a third of
all projects come up for review each year and this presents the
opportunity to support new projects. In a climate of financial
stringency the Urban Programme provides the main opportunity for new
developments. The Council have used the Programme until 1980 primarily to support developments in the seven area initiatives and
GEAR. Thereafter, an increased proportion of the Programme was
allocated to the 45 areas and to client based projects, particularly
in the fields of addiction, the single homeless and offenders. The
Council supported projects which were mainly sponsored by its own
departments although voluntary organisations and community groups
have been increasingly important agents for the Urban Programme,
particularly since the inception of the Community Development Committee. The Scottish Development Department (SDD) changed the
balance of the Programme earlier when they introduced Circular 7/81
which outlined new criteria and priorities. As far as the Council
is concerned there are three main changes. There is to be a shift
in the Programme towards voluntary organisations or community based
projects. Projects must be area based in line with SDD policy
(SDD, 1978) which is to target and discriminate towards areas of
deprivation and greater emphasis will be given to wealth creating
type projects. Whilst it is always necessary to keep in perspective
the small size of the Urban Programme compared with the Council's
mainline budget (about one per cent) the constant paring at departmental budgets has meant that the Urban Programme has fulfilled a
vital role in positive discrimination throughout the region and will
continue to do so.

Poverty

The Council has little or no direct influence upon the incidence of
poverty and it is with regret that during the five years of the
strategy, the number of people living at or below the state poverty
line has increased significantly. Moreover, there has been a

lowering of the state poverty line as benefits are no longer linked
to the standard of living. In a region like Strathclyde this has a
marked effect upon the local economy. The action taken by the
Council has largely focused on the creation of a Welfare Rights
team within Social Work. Dealing with individual clients, the 40
Welfare Rights staff now in post have made an important contribution
towards ensuring that many thousands of people in the region are
receiving their entitlements. At the wider level campaigns have
been mounted to challenge the practices of both the DHSS and the
Fuel Boards. The school clothing allowances and the ending of many
discretionary payments have particularly affected Strathclyde.
Welfare benefits are a vital part of any sustained attack on deprivation and with a growing number of the population dependent on benefits and if, as seems likely, unemployment is a permanent feature
of society, then the financial penalties must be reduced if the
quality of life is to be improved.

Community Development

No longstanding progress can be made without involving local communities in identifying and helping overcome the difficulties facing
them. When the Red Book recognised this it pointed towards the need
for a far more effective community development policy by the Council. A new committee was established in 1980 to oversee Community
Development. The community work staffing complements in Community
Education and Social Work have been considerably increased and 19
Area Development Teams have now been inaugurated to pursue a wide
variety of community goals in various parts cf the region. The resources made available to community groups have increased and now
include Urban Programme, Community Council grants as well as Education and Social Work grants. The Council are presently examining
the rationalisation of all grants and decentralisation of some funds
to individual areas. A further problem confronting almost all deprived communities is the lack of available premises. Although the
Council has supported community flats to provide local meeting
places they cannot support the many activities that take place in
communities. Council premises, in particular schools, are a local
resource capable of far greater use. The problem in releasing
schools for community use remains intractable. A combination of
diminishing resources and the attitude of some head teachers and
janitors militates against the use of such buildings. The Council
wants to ensure that maximum use is made of school facilities to
the benefit of the whole community. Increased unemployment and the
large fall in school rolls mean that daytime use also needs to be
part of any future developments.

REVIEW OF THE POLICY

A major problem of the strategy is that the deprivation policy was
often unspecific, not understood nor accepted by some staff and has
been implemented imperfectly. Two major ambiguities of the strategy
are worth outlining:

    i)   by calling for positive discrimination and at the same
        time making available Urban Programme, the Urban Programme
        has been seen as the principal means of discrimination and
        less attention has been paid to redirecting mainline pro-
        grammes;
   ii)   three of the principal concerns - poverty, employment and
        housing - are outwith the direct control of the Council
        and any significant progress requires advocacy action.

On the positive side, the strategy is widely known by many fieldworkers, voluntary organisations and community groups. The Urban Programme has almost entirely been targetted, extra staff have been redistributed to the more difficult areas. The area initiatives have challenged traditional ways of working and given useful experience on community development. A Community Development Committee has been formed and community services have been greatly enhanced. On the debit side, deprivation has increased, departmental expenditure has been continuously decreased making it more difficult to redirect resources; traditional methods of working survive often to the detriment of areas in need and the attitudes of many staff prevent the implementation of the spirit of the deprivation policy. Too often staff hide behind the rules and regulations, are unwilling to use initiative, or to question existing practice; an attitude which will deepen the sense of rejection already there and reduce the chances of local participation.

Positive discrimination requires great commitment in the current financial climate of Local Government, and so far the APTs have been protected from the cuts which are already hitting many services. But even this protection is insufficient in areas taking the brunt of the current economic recession. Increased unemployment has consequences for the social wellbeing and health of individuals. Marital breakdown, more children coming into care, more truancy, alcoholism and poor health all are associated with increased unemployment and require in a just society a growth in services to cope with the problems. Thus whilst it can be claimed with some success that staffing levels in the fields of education, police and social work have improved in the APTs, the services may not have improved simply because of the greater intensity of the problems. The steady drop in the crime rate in the late 1970s, particularly in the APTs has since been reversed despite the fact that staffing levels are as high as ever at the moment.

In many ways the policies to date have relied upon the action of the above departments but in themselves these departments are incapable of resolving the basic problems which confront the Region's deprived communities. Any list of priorities produced by a community would highlight five major issues as jobs, family income, housing, transport and health and with the exception of transport these are mainly outwith the direct control of the Council.

The Council have opened major new transport systems such as the modernised underground and Clyderail and have introduced a travel card for the elderly and handicapped which has been a great success. On the other hand, the reduction of public transport services and the continuing high cost of public transport for families and households living on state benefits means that transport is a major problem in many communities including the APTs, where car ownership is low. The recent 'Quality of Life for the Unemployed' initiatives undertaken by the Council have frequently foundered on the difficulties of the unemployed travelling to leisure facilities because of the high cost of public transport. Community transport has been seen to be the answer to the APT transport difficulties. But it can only play a limited role and the real answer must be in re-thinking existing public transport services. Other problems frequently highlighted by communities are the poor state of pavements in the region. For the vast majority of people living in APTs pavements are the principal channel of transport yet they receive low priority in budgets.

Given the presence of the Scottish Development Agency and the status of the whole of Strathclyde as a special Development Area, the Council has allocated only limited resources to programmes for the creation and support of employment. It is inevitable therefore that the Council has had only a limited influence on the economic development of the region. Although the Council has tried to attract investment from all sources it is recognised that this will not solve the underlying problem of the region's economy. The alternative philosophy of supporting indigenous industry and encouraging local enterprise has been pursued within the limited resources of the Industrial Development Unit. New enterprise workshops have been established, joint factory developments started, Integrated Workforce Units have been created, and a counselling service has been provided for small businesses. In recent months the Council has made progress towards establishing Enterprise Trust Funds and has submitted a scheme through the European Social Fund for a recruitment employment scheme.

Not all these developments have been in the APTs although a policy has now been agreed with the SDA to concentrate future developments in economic priority areas which relate to some of the APTs. The Council also controls employment opportunity through its own role as employer of 107 000 staff. Although this level has been dropping, there remains considerable scope for employing para professional staff which could benefit the APT areas where fewer people have educational qualifications. The fact remains that the SDA has been regarded as the senior partner in these fields although it is apparent that the brief of the SDA precludes support to high risk enterprises, community employment initiatives and Council funded companies. It is in these fields that the Council is beginning to re-examine its strategy. Whatever developments take place it is unlikely that there will be a significant reduction in unemployment in the APTs, where current unemployment rates exceed 30 per cent, this requires other measures aimed at providing services for the unemployed.

Recent Policy Changes

Within the last year the deprivation policy has shifted in four main areas:-

i)   establishment of Divisional Deprivation Groups
ii)   review of the APTs
iii) Urban Programme
iv)   Community development

Deprivation Groups

Early in 1981, it was agreed that Member/Officer Deprivation Groups should be established at the region and in each division. These groups were established in recognition of the key role which officials at divisional level played in interpreting and carrying out the Council's strategy locally. The regional group has a wider remit of review and policy formulation. It is able to debate in greater depth, with a wider representation, the deprivation strategy issues which could not be accommodated in the tight timetable of the Multiple Deprivation Sub-Committee, which gives most of its time to the Urban Programme.

Review of Areas for Priority Treatment

It was the arguments presented by communities and staff in certain parts of the region, that conditions in areas had changed through demolition, improvements, house allocation policies and economic circumstances, that led to the need to widen the range of priority areas as economic and social conditions deteriorated in the region. The areas which were originally selected in 1976 using 1971 data were re-examined and new priority areas have been defined. The new analysis was based upon demographic indicators, certain departmental indicators, and in some districts housing information. As a result 75 areas are now designated as Areas for Priority Treatment. Most of these areas were contained within the original 114 areas but there are a few new areas.

The 1981 Census will allow the Council to re-examine the whole of the region at enumeration district level. This will enable the problems of the rural areas to be re-examined and for policies to be developed to tackle the smaller pockets of deprivation which are often outwith the existing APT areas.

Urban Programme

Following the SDD Circular in February 1981, the Council undertook a review of the operation of the Urban Programme. Responsibility for the preparation of the Programme was vested with Divisional Deprivation Groups. This ensures member involvement, joint working between departments, and more feasible projects being brought to committee. Each Divisional Group now receives an allocation of Urban Programme according to measures of need in that division. The Council has also produced new guidelines which endorse the SDD Circular in making an increased allocation available to community groups and voluntary organisations through the Community Development Committee, and provide criteria for projects. Eligibility was extended to cover the new 75 APTs and projects for client groups provided they were adequately justified. Two separate funds were also established - minor projects, under £1500 and measures to assist the unemployed. Both of these pools of grant are disbursed from the Community Development Committee and enables a far quicker turn round than the normal procedure of submitting applications to the SDD for approval.

Community Development

Since the establishment of the Community Development Committee a number of changes have been put in motion. Primarily the Committee are actively encouraging community groups, evaluating a wide range of developments throughout the Region and most important examining ways in which decisions can be decentralised to local groups. Five community conferences were held in March, 1982 to enable community groups in each Division to exert an influence on future policy changes.

Other Developments

Two other developments have been significant in reinforcing the deprivation policy: Member/Officer Groups and Social Work Needs and Resources documents. They have developed a policy framework for client groups and adhere to the deprivation policy of trying to adjust priorities to meet real needs.

a) Member/Officer Groups

The first Member/Officer Groups were established early in 1977 and can be seen as an allied development to the deprivation policy. The Red Book highlighted the insensitivity of many services, the lack of co-ordination and lack of corporate planning. The Member/Officer Groups have provided a mechanism whereby services for client groups can be investigated and future services better planned to reflect priorities of need and improve methods of service delivery. The Member/Officer Groups have also harnessed the latent energy of many staff and have led to a better understanding by the authority of how and where services should be delivered. During the last five years nine such groups have been established and they represent an important part of the Council's commitment to improve and refine services particularly to those most in need.

The groups have covered:-

Child care
Mentally handicapped
Ex offenders
Addiction
Physically handicapped
Post compulsory education and training
The first two years of secondary education
Children's panels
Under fives

b) Social work needs and resources

Existing Social Work services have been compared with the relative
needs in each division to provide a framework of priorities. Whilst
this analysis is independent of the areas of deprivation, it confirms the need for services to be improved in the APT areas. The
second round of these studies were available in May, 1982 and cover
the whole region.

CHANGING CONTEXT

During the five years since the 'Multiple Deprivation' document was
produced, Strathclyde has witnessed dramatic changes which require
the relevance of the deprivation strategy to be reassessed. The
most significant changes are to the economy of the region. Unemployment has increased from ten per cent in 1976 to twenty per cent in
1981. Youth unemployment which was only beginning to surface in
1976 now confronts 50 per cent of school leavers. Many major firms
have closed during the past two years, and despite localised suc-
cesses by the SDA, the underlying trend in the region is one of continuing decline. Allied to the high unemployment rate, Strathclyde
is more dependent on Social Security than any other region in
Britain. The consequences of recent changes to benefit levels is to
reduce the purchasing power or more pertinent the basic standard of
living of about a quarter of the region's population. Yet an underlying cause of deprivation is financial poverty so that the extent
of relative deprivation is spreading in the region. Nowhere in
Britain is the effect of unemployment and poverty more marked than
in Strathclyde which makes it essential for the Council to pursue
vigorously actions aimed at ameliorating the dehumanising effects of
unemployment and debating conventional attitudes towards the work
ethic, which certainly within Strathclyde, seem irrelevant to large
sections of the population. There are other social trends which
reinforce the growth of disadvantage in the region. The number of
pensioners continues to increase particularly in the older age
groups, the number of single parent families has increased dramatically and coupled with the recent increase in the birth rate, there
are far more young children in single parent families. Equally important the number of school leavers continues at its peak level
coinciding with the big decrease in job availability. These social
changes serve to further increase the number of people dependent on
state benefits and public services, and make it more important for
the Council's services to be properly targetted.
  Superimposed on the economic and social changes outlined above
is the environment within local government. The past five years
have not been years of expansion as in the 1960s or early 1970s.
Indeed over the period 1976 to 1981 there has been a net decline in
resources available to local authorities. The Council's mainline
revenue expenditure has been reduced by two per cent over this period
and capital expenditure has been reduced by 33 per cent. Increasing

demands for services necessitated by the social and economic change are confronted with departments having to make net savings in services. In consequence it has not been possible to develop more appropriate services as quickly as necessary and in many cases no improvements have been made.

Within limited and declining resources both now and for the foreseeable future, Strathclyde will need to shift existing services and perhaps accept that universal services will have to be sacrificed to meet the recognised priorities. This in turn will require the Council to re-examine its statutory obligations and debate the future nature of local government, rather than acceding unquestioningly to control from central government. Only a willingness to innovate and forge ahead with appropriate local policies will enable the Council to keep abreast of the changes which are reinforcing the need for a stronger deprivation policy. In this sense the Council needs to acknowledge the changing nature of societal attitudes and goals. The relevance of education, family living patterns, the importance of work, and the growth of leisure time all threaten the traditional nature of Local Government and require open and searching questions to be asked of current services. The Member/ Officer Groups have begun to do this and the new committee machinery, whether Community Development, Divisional Groups, or the expertise developed by traditional committees such as Social Work, all represent ways in which the Council is trying to keep abreast of change. All these events pose a different political, economic and social backcloth than five years ago. It is crucial that as a concerned Council we should take the opportunity to re-examine our mechanisms to cope with those changes. However, even without such challenges, the problems of poverty and the insensitivity of many services remain and must be tackled.

OUTSTANDING ISSUES

Although progress has been made it is evident that the strategy can be strengthened. The broad directions contained in the Red Book were insufficient guidance to detailed policy making and implementation. There is a need to provide a checklist of targets for policy implementation. Equally the original intention of 'putting our own house in order' was probably correct but on reviewing the growing deprivation in many parts of the region there is a need for the Council to take up the issues with Central Government, District Councils and other agencies if it is to do other than take ameliorative action. The key problem remains and has deteriorated - unemployment. The Council must decide whether the creation of jobs by itself will significantly reduce the level of unemployment or whether the 'collapse of work' is now a reality. If so the Council needs perhaps to make a commitment to providing services which acknowledge that a significant proportion of the economically active population require a different type of local authority service than provided hitherto. Recent developments with the SDA are indicative of the Council's concern to explore new economic initiatives.

Within the strict ambit of the Council's activities there is a need to widen the perspective of what is meant by the deprivation policy. There is a tendency for education and social work to be regarded as the front line attack against deprivation. There is a considerable contribution that can be made by other departments by either positive discrimination or greater flexibility in methods of operation. Such changes are already being pursued through the Urban Programme but require wider application by departments. The relationship of the Council's capital programmes to the strategy also merits further investigation. At a time when capital programmes have been cut by a third, it is important that programmes are

targetted to eradicating inequalities in the region. There has
been a tendency for infrastructure investment to be used to meet
statutory obligations such as servicing greenfield housing developments. This has often been at the expense of replacing or renewing
outworn infrastructure in the region. The replacement of lead water
pipes and pavement repairs are but two examples of how investment
could be redirected. Overall there is evidence that departmental
programmes are still drawn up independently of the Council's
strategy.

A great deal remains to be done to inculcate staff with the
knowledge of policies. Throughout the region there are far too many
examples of implementation falling down because the implementer did
not know the policy, or saw it as outwith his traditional remit.
Lines of communication must be shortened and messages must be made
clearer. The initiatives have shown that many fieldworkers are
thwarted in their attempts to innovate by the confused and often
contradictory advice received from their superiors. A further problem stems from the loss of many excellent fieldworkers into senior
positions with the result that the service on the ground suffers.
Whilst no policy can ever overcome the attitude of staff, a great
deal must be done towards the achievement of better communication
of policy and overcoming the intransigence of some staff towards the
acceptance or implementation of Council policies. There is a great
deal of scope for decentralisation of decision making within the
region involving local members and which would effectively bring
into play a wider range of staff. Already community chests have
been established and other grants are disbursed on a local level.
Decentralisation of minor budgets to communities has many virtues,
not least the transfer of responsibilities to the community. If the
Council can release its hold on these purses then a great deal will
have been achieved to making services more relevant and engendering
self help within communities.

The problem of an area based strategy remains; undoubtedly there
are disadvantaged communities excluded from the analysis and some
of these will be in rural areas. Whilst this can be examined
through the 1981 Census, the Council must make clear what priority
should be attached to these areas, and importantly perhaps, must
identify the areas where services must be cut to facilitate an improvement of services to the deprived rural areas as well as the
urban areas. Whilst a great deal has been done to monitor conditions
in various areas, it is only recently that research into the effec-
tiveness of policy has begun to be carried out. The Social Work
Needs and Resources surveys are one example. The Council must ensure that proper research and evaluation programmes are established
to test the success of its policies. Inevitably this means that
standards and targets for services must be set. Finally, there is
the question of other agencies. Any attack on deprivation depends
upon housing, health, income and environment. The next phase of
the strategy must enshrine a firmer commitment from the authorities
controlling these services but as elsewhere with the Council's
services, targets must be agreed and monitored if real progress is
to be made.

REFERENCES

Black, Sir D. 1981. *Inequalities in Health*.

Holterman, S. 1975. *Census Indicators of Urban Deprivation*. DoE Working Note No. 6.

Scottish Development Department, 1978. *Area Based Policies Approach to Urban Deprivation*.

Strathclyde Regional Council, 1976a. *Regional Report*.

Strathclyde Regional Council, 1976b. *Urban Deprivation*.

Strathclyde Regional Council, 1976c. *Multiple Deprivation*.

Strathclyde Regional Council, 1980. *Social Needs and Social Work Resources*.

Strathclyde Regional Council, 1982. *Demographic Indicators 1976-78*.

Wedge, P. and Prosser, H. 1973. *Born to Fail?* (Arrow Books).

West Central Scotland Plan Team, 1974. *Consultative Draft Report*.

Discussant's Comments

Brian Dicks

The papers by Gordon and Danson analyse at length, generally and with specific reference to the West of Scotland, the substance of the term deprivation, a condition acknowledged as one extreme in a continuum of physical and socio-economic experiences by which researchers judge the 'well-being' and 'lifestyle' of individuals and societies. Strictly defined, deprivation is the act of prevention or dispossession leading to circumstances currently portrayed by the negative images in such cliches as 'the haves and have-nots', 'the privileged and underprivileged' and 'the affluent and needy'.
These traditionally counterposed values, common to societies throughout history, have led to considerable abstract and subjective arguments that attempt to qualify and measure the degree of deprivation. In their endeavours to approach the problem objectively social scientists have applied a variety of nationally available indices that, mathematically manipulated, define the position of an individual, family or society in terms of a graduated socioeconomic ladder, negative deviations from the norm indicating the scale of deprivation. Gordon rightly argues that the major difficulties in such an academic exercise relate to the multidimensional character of deprivation and also to its marked spatial variation, the latter appearing in contexts ranging from purely local settings to those involving profound regional and national inequalities.
It must also be acknowledged that any analysis of deprivation is further obstructed by the now common reliance on such abstractions as 'a sense of well-being' and 'the quality of life' as providing meaningful evaluations of the problem. Though obviously critical factors both are the highly subjective summaries of values and ideals derived from an individual's or a society's past experience, present condition and future aspiration.
Both papers stress that in Britain in the 1980s it is the employment ratio that forms the fundamental component in the deprivation syndrome and the principal cause of existing life-style dichotomies. Danson's view that the West of Scotland unenviably portrays the greatest incidence of multiple deprivation in Britain is readily supported when local and regional statistics are compared with national averages. At the focus of the problem is the City of Glasgow where current high unemployment levels compound the complex of social and environmental problems inherited from earlier decades and with which the image of the city is invariably associated. Significantly, other indices, particularly those relating to diet, health and the incidence of acute and chronic disease, also indicate the West of Scotland and much of the Central Belt as being Britain's most onerous region. The increasing rise in crime rates, vandalism, drug addiction and alcoholism, in part the concomitants of high unemployment, add to the collective image of social degradation.
Danson recognises the failure of Central Government to remedy the West of Scotland problem, the current Westminster policies being seen to accentuate rather than abate the 'circles of virtues and vice'. There seems little doubt that such processes, if remaining unchecked, will foster a polarised society split socially, economically and morally between the employed classes and the

jobless. The Deprivation Strategy, inaugurated in 1975 by Strathclyde Regional Council, must be viewed as one of Britain's most
ambitious examples of regional self-help. In many ways the success
of the Strategy has been the way in which its own deficiencies have
been highlighted by drawing attention to the need for further extensive research and a critical and constructive evaluation of its
programmes, especially in the light of reduced budgets. Importantly,
the Region has fully recognised the spatial dimension of the deprivation problem by earmarking Areas for Priority Treatment in
which it has worked with Glasgow District Council (on, for example,
the GEAR project) and with supra-regional bodies such as the SDA.
Over the last decade practical application of the self-help philosophy has considerably improved the City of Glasgow's urban fabric
and current policies are actively involved in promoting a new self-
confidence as the image of the city, not least in the eyes of its
inhabitants, continues to improve. A major contributing factor in
growing self-confidence has been the District Council's policy of
Area Management which is seen as an important step towards the
effective decentralisation of power to local communities. Glasgow
can quote a number of neighbourhoods where environmental quality
has greatly improved and local pride returned as a result of self-
help community action.

Though progress has been made in the deprivation battle, the key
problem in Glasgow and the West of Scotland remains unemployment and
its demoralising effects on the region as a whole. Its rate continues to rise sharply, largely as a reflection of closures and
cut-backs in the traditional, older established industries. The
present situation raises serious issues about the region's entire
developmental process and the concomitant dilemmas are highly
charged with social and political values. Flexible and innovative
policies, generated within the region have produced significant
ameliorating results, yet Central Government's policy of maximising
total development at the price of spatial inequalities has to be
seen as a fundamental cause of the West of Scotland problem.

Chapter 5

Revealed Preferences and Residential

Environmental Quality

Michael Pacione

The quality of the residential environment is a basic component of every person's definition of life quality. Consequently residential environmental quality has emerged as a key part of the general debate on the quality of life in the industrialised world. In Scotland, as a result of a building surge in the post-war era and the demolition of unfit tenement structures, the majority of the population are now accommodated in local authority housing. Progress has been such that, in the major cities, most of the sub-standard private housing has been removed or is undergoing rehabilitation. As a result attention is increasingly being focussed on the quality of the residential environment in the worst parts of the council stock.

Public housing authorities throughout Britain have attempted to establish quantitative definitions of residential environmental quality to aid planning and housing policy formulation. Two factors have hampered progress however. The first is that traditional indicators of housing quality (such as possession of a bath, hot water supply, and inside toilet) are not relevant to post-war council housing which is generally well provided with standard amenities. It is clear, however, that the quality of life in some council estates is adversely affected by factors such as overcrowding, physical dereliction, poor service provision, and vandalism; and there is strong evidence to support the view that such public housing is both physically inadequate and instrumental in precipitating social and psychological problems. A second limitation of traditional indicators of residential quality is that none of the measures, on which planning and housing policies are normally based, give serious attention to the views and preferences of residents. The limitations of employing only objective physical measures of housing quality or normative evaluation systems (Burisch, 1979) which depend on the judgements of 'expert' observers have been exposed by several authors including Abrams (1973), and Andrews and Withey (1976) who point out that it is people's perceptions of their own well being or lack of well being that ultimately define the quality of their lives. A similar view was expressed by Francescato (1980) who concluded that the most likely means of achieving better housing is 'based on a much more widespread use of scientific research into residents' perceptions and particularly into residents' satisfaction with a variety of residential options'.

There is a need therefore for a measure of residential environmental quality which reflects the views of residents and which can be applied to modern local authority housing areas. The present investigation set out to identify the major components of a satisfactory residential environment and to assess their importance in

a measure of residential environmental quality, with particular
reference to a deprived council estate.

STUDY AREA

The Ferguslie Park estate in Paisley is a policy-created ghetto in
which the high levels of rent arrears and unemployment, the rapid
turnover of tenants, rampant vandalism and the social stigma associated with the estate are the result of a council policy of deliber-
ately collecting difficult families together. As Figure 5.1 indicates, plotting the previous address of residents of Ferguslie
Park reveals the restricted spatial mobility of households in this
part of the public housing system.
    The boundaries of the estate are clearly demarcated by industry,
railway lines and vacant land (Figure 5.2). Building took place in
three main phases; a number of general needs houses, mainly cottage
flats, built during the 1920s; tenement blocks of flats built in
the 1930s for rehousing from slum clearance areas under the terms
of the Housing (Scotland) Act 1930; and post-war houses, the
latest of which were built in the 1960s. Of an original total of
3536 houses, 2586 remained standing in April 1982 and only 2200

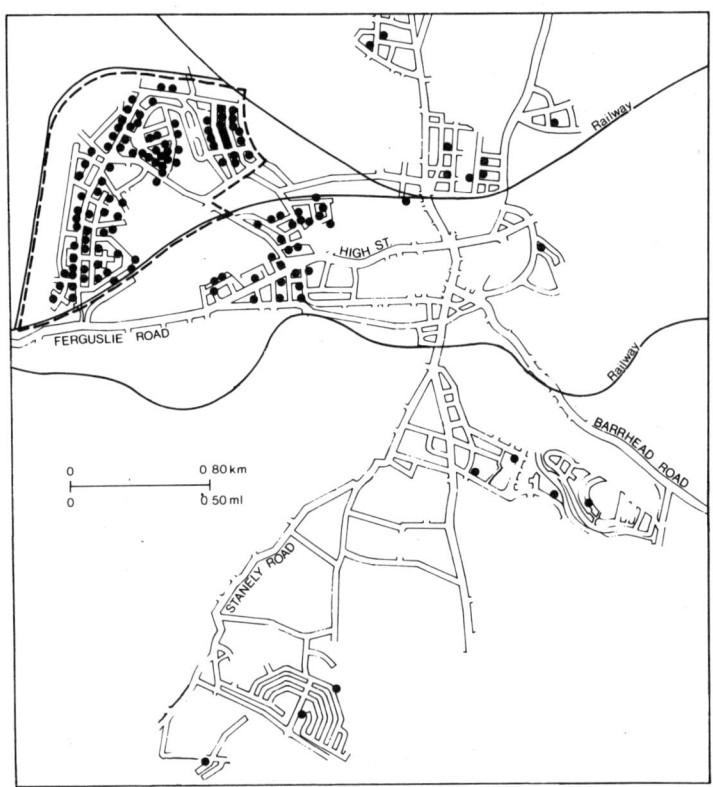

Figure 5.1 Origins of residents of Ferguslie Park

52

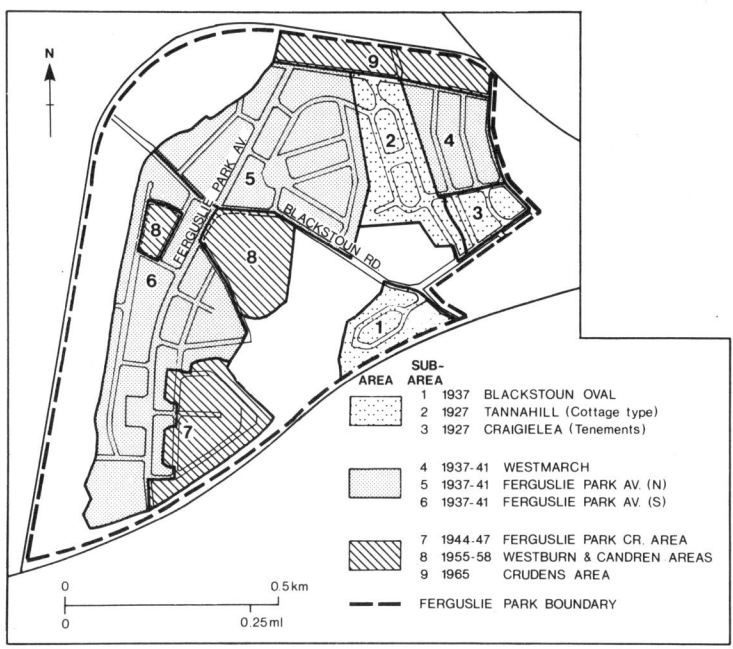

Figure 5.2   The study area boundaries: Ferguslie Park

Table 5.1   Comparative indicators of deprivation

INDICATOR	FERGUSLIE PARK	CLYDESIDE CONURBATION	GREAT BRITAIN
% total population aged 0-14	38	26	23
% households with 6 or more persons	22	10	6
% households living at > 1.5 p.p.r.	14	11	2
% e.a. males unemployed and seeking work	22	9	5
% e.a. and retired males in S.E.G.11 (unskilled manual)	29	12	8
% households with no car	89	68	54

were occupied. As English (1976) has shown 'conditions within the estate vary considerably; whilst the oldest and newest houses are generally in reasonable condition, those built during the 1930s are often in an appalling state and some of them are unlet. Though there are enclaves of relatively desirable housing, most of the estate has a poor reputation and is accepted locally as being the least popular in the district'. Table 5.1 portrays the depth of deprivation in Ferguslie Park by presenting a number of diagnostic indicators for the estate, Clydeside and Great Britain.

CRITERIA OF RESIDENTIAL ENVIRONMENTAL QUALITY

There is no generally accepted definition of what constitutes a decent home and a suitable living environment. As Duncan (1971) pointed out, although the presence of certain basic facilities might be sought by all, some families have no need of a garden while others enjoy tending a large area; some wish to live close to a town centre for the convenience it brings while others will accept a longer journey to work or shop if they can live in more open surroundings. Francescato (1980) found that residents place great value on visual and auditory privacy, on the opportunity to personalise the dwelling unit, on a variety of shapes in buildings and landscape, on easy access to the ground and to their parked cars, on an enclosed piece of ground that one can call one's own, and on the small size of a development. Other physical factors found to influence housing satisfaction are structural type (Rent and Rent, 1978), tenure type, nature of physical surroundings and access to services and facilities (Marans and Rodgers, 1974).

Personal factors which may affect residential satisfaction include previous housing experience (Fried and Gleicher, 1961), the degree of integration of the individual into society (Tauber and Levin, 1971), the individual's reference group (Merton, 1968), the person's socio-psychological attitude towards society in general (Gans, 1967), people's social customs and traditions (Duncan, 1971) and the individual's aspiration level (Campbell and Converse, 1972). It is virtually impossible however to incorporate these psychological dimensions into a generally applicable measure of residential environmental quality and most studies have concentrated instead on the characteristics of the house and neighbourhood occupied by particular population groups.

In the present investigation the main criteria employed by residents to evaluate their residential environment were identified by means of a review of previous attempts to assess residential environmental quality (e.g. Sanoff and Sawhney, 1972; Troy, 1973; Hall, 1976; Hoinville, 1971; Michelson, 1977) and a questionnaire-interview with a random sample of 150 households in Ferguslie Park.

The questionnaire survey revealed that 60 per cent of respondents expressed a wish to leave the estate (Figure 5.3). When questioned about their motives for wishing to move away the greatest proportion (19.2 per cent) referred to the poor general environment and to dirty streets and unkempt gardens in particular (Table 5.2). Another major 'push' factor was the size of house occupied which often failed to correspond with household needs. House type was also a major source of dissatisfaction with 11.5 per cent reporting a dislike of tenement life and a preference for a house with their 'own front door and garden'. One householder in ten cited vandalism and acts of crime, such as house-breaking, as reasons for their desire to move. Other important push factors were the bad reputation and social stigma attached to the estate, and the conviction that it was not a good environment in which to raise children.

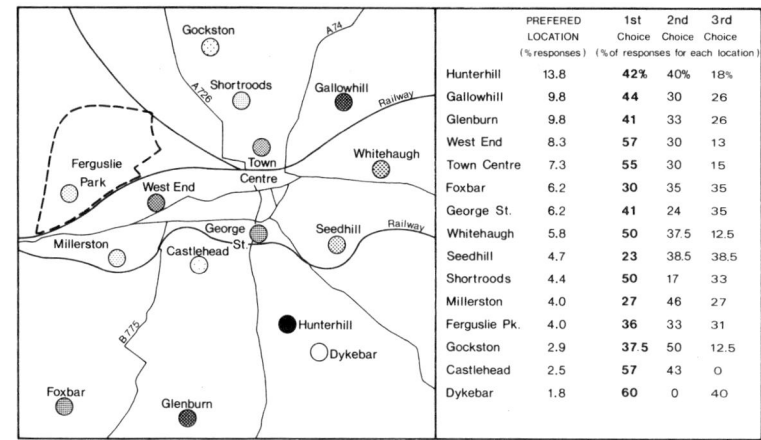

PREFERED LOCATION (% responses)	1st Choice	2nd Choice	3rd Choice
		(% of responses for each location)	
Hunterhill	13.8	42%	40%	18%
Gallowhill	9.8	44	30	26
Glenburn	9.8	41	33	26
West End	8.3	57	30	13
Town Centre	7.3	55	30	15
Foxbar	6.2	30	35	35
George St.	6.2	41	24	35
Whitehaugh	5.8	50	37.5	12.5
Seedhill	4.7	23	38.5	38.5
Shortroods	4.4	50	17	33
Millerston	4.0	27	46	27
Ferguslie Pk.	4.0	36	33	31
Gockston	2.9	37.5	50	12.5
Castlehead	2.5	57	43	0
Dykebar	1.8	60	0	40

Figure 5.3   Residential preferences of Ferguslie Park council housing tenants

Table 5.2   Residents' reasons for wishing to move from Ferguslie Park

FACTOR	n	%	FACTOR	n	%
House size	21	11.5	Anti-social neighbours	6	3.3
House type	21	11.5	Bad for children	15	8.2
House structural condition	10	5.5	Isolation	5	2.8
Vandalism and crime	18	9.9	Lack of local facilities	7	3.9
Poor environment	35	19.2	Family	10	5.5
Estate reputation	16	8.8	Other	18	9.9

The combination of research review and field survey provided a comprehensive list of over 100 criteria which could be applied to the assessment of residential environmental quality in the study area.   This was reduced to the 49 variables shown in Table 5.3 by amalgamating measures which differed only in terms of semantics. Each of the 150 respondents was asked to evaluate their own residential situation on each of the 49 measures, using a seven point equal interval scale.   Evaluations of the neighbourhood in general and of the dwelling as a whole were also obtained by calculating the mean of two questions on each theme located at different points in the interview schedule.

Table 5.3 Criteria of residential environmental quality

VAR 01 How would you rate your neighbourhood/this area as a place to live
VAR 02 The time it takes to go to the local shops
VAR 03 The goods and services you can buy locally
VAR 04 Journey time to work
VAR 05 Ease of reaching city centre shops
VAR 06 The distance to school for children
VAR 07 The standard of local schools
VAR 08 The distance to church
VAR 09 The distance to your friends and relatives
VAR 10 The distance to entertainments
VAR 11 Your access to open countryside
VAR 12 Availability of parks and play areas
VAR 13 The public transport service
VAR 14 Availability of health services
VAR 15 The amount of traffic on the streets
VAR 16 The noise from traffic
VAR 17 The risk of a traffic accident
VAR 18 Car parking facilities
VAR 19 The general appearance of the area
VAR 20 The amount of trees and greenery nearby
VAR 21 The tidiness of the streets and surrounding areas
VAR 22 The amount of smoke and dust in the air
VAR 23 The standard of maintenance of the communal area
VAR 24 Your neighbours
VAR 25 The rubbish collection service
VAR 26 The standard of street lighting
VAR 27 The upkeep of roads, paths and pavements
VAR 28 The fire service available
VAR 29 About walking alone at night
VAR 30 The level of vandalism
VAR 31 The security of your home from theft
VAR 32 The availability of safe areas for young children to play
VAR 33 The nuisance from roving dogs
VAR 34 The way the council and housing department attends to your complaints

Table 5.3 continued

VAR 35   The amount of influence you can have on what goes on in your area
VAR 36   The reputation of your area
VAR 37   This house/flat as a place to live
VAR 38   The number of rooms you have
VAR 39   The size and layout of rooms
VAR 40   The outside appearance of your house/flat
VAR 41   The amount of outside space you have for your own use
VAR 42   The standard of building and internal repair
VAR 43   The amount of noise from neighbours
VAR 44   The amount of noise from outside
VAR 45   The privacy you have from neighbours
VAR 46   The level of rents
VAR 47   The efficiency of the heating system in winter
VAR 48   The cost of heating your home in winter
VAR 49   Problems of damp or condensation
VAR 50   The amount of sunlight you receive
VAR 51   The view from your living room

IDENTIFYING THE COMPONENTS OF A SATISFACTORY
RESIDENTIAL ENVIRONMENT

The primary data set consisted of measurements on 49 variables for
150 households. A correlation matrix was first constructed to
examine the degree of association among the variables. This then
formed the basis for an R-type principal components analysis. This
procedure was employed to reduce the size of the initial data set
and to extract a smaller set of components to account for most of
the variance in the original data. The principal components methodology has been employed extensively in geographic research and the
mechanics and algebra of the technique have been well described by
several authors (Harman, 1960; Johnston, 1978). A varimax rotation
of the initial component matrix produced nine components with well
defined structures, and which together accounted for 77.4 per cent
of the variance. The character of the nine components is indicated
in Table 5.4 which shows the most important (> 0.30) loadings for
each.
    The first component, accounting for 28.7 per cent of the total
variance, loaded highly on variables 15 (amount of traffic on the
streets), 16 (noise from traffic), 17 (risk of a traffic accident)
and 44 (amount of noise from outside) and was clearly a measure of
traffic problems. Component II loaded highly on variables 40 (outside appearance of dwelling), 42 (standard of building and internal
repair), 47 (efficiency of heating system in winter) and 49 (problems of damp or condensation). This was interpreted as a measure
of housing condition, with high component scores indicative of more
satisfactory conditions. Component III exhibited high positive
loadings on variables 19 (general appearance of area), 20 (amount
of trees and greenery nearby), 21 (tidiness of streets and

surrounding areas), 22 (amount of smoke and dust in the air), and
51 (view from living room) and was considered to be an indicator of
the quality of the external environment. The loadings of greatest
magnitude on component IV were related to variables 30 (level of
vandalism), 31 (security of home from theft), 33 (nuisance from
roving dogs) and 36 (reputation of area). This component, which
accounted for seven per cent of the variance was most closely associated with the concept of 'anti-social activity'. The characteristic structure of component V was based on its high association with
variables 24 (neighbours), 43 (amount of noise from neighbours) and
45 (privacy from neighbours). The structure of the component matrix
also enabled a clear interpretation to be placed on components VI -
IX and these are shown in Table 5.4.

The component structure confirmed the intuitive conclusion that
the residential environment comprises two separate but related
elements - i.e. the dwelling unit and the surrounding neighbourhood.
It was necessary, therefore, a) to identify the major components of
residential quality for each of these elements of the residential
environment, and b) to determine the relative contribution of individual components to the residents' overall satisfaction with
i) the neighbourhood and ii) the dwelling.

The neighbourhood

A principal components analysis was carried out with variables
02 - 36 of the original data set; being those particularly concerned
with the environment surrounding the dwelling (Table 5.3). Twelve
components with eigenvalues greater than unity were found to account
for 65.2 per cent of the variance (Table 5.5). As expected a number
of components found in the analysis of the aggregate set of variables also emerged in the separate analysis of the 'neighbourhood'
variables. Thus components I, III, IV and VI in the aggregate
analysis also appeared at the sub-group level with only slight
changes in the variables with high loadings in each case. Of equal
significance, however, were the components not reproduced at this
level as well as any new components to emerge. Component VIII of
the aggregate analysis (standard of public services), for example,
did not feature at the sub-group level; and component III was divided
into two more detailed indicators measuring the 'cleanliness of the
physical environment' (Component II) and the 'greenness' of the
environment (Component VII). In addition, two new components were
created. The first, component V, loaded highly on variables 05
(ease of reaching city centre shops), 04 (journey time to work),
10 (distance to entertainments), 03 (goods and services available
locally), and 14 (availability of health services) and could be
interpreted as a measure of accessibility. The second, (Component
VI), with high loadings on variable 9 (distance to friends and relatives) and variable 24 (neighbours) was less clearly structured
but could be regarded as an indicator of 'quality of social contacts'.

The dwelling

To isolate the major elements of dwelling unit satisfaction variables 38 - 51 were subjected to a separate principal components
analysis. Five components were extracted to explain 61.9 per cent
of the variance. A varimax rotation produced the component structures shown in Table 5.6. Components I - IV were readily comparable
with components II, IX, V, and VII respectively of the aggregate
analysis (c.f. tables 5.4 and 5.6). The fifth component to emerge
loaded highly on variables 48 (cost of heating in winter), 46 (level
of rent) and 47 (efficiency of heating in winter) and was interpreted as a measure of 'house running costs'.

Table 5.4 Component structures: aggregate analysis

Component I: (Traffic problems)		Component II: (House condition)	
VAR 15 Amount of traffic on streets	C.89762	VAR 40 Outside appearance of house/flat	0.46743
VAR 16 Noise from traffic	0.85087	VAR 42 Standard of building and internal repair	0.69176
VAR 17 Risk of a traffic accident	0.75457	VAR 47 Efficiency of heating system in winter	0.36727
VAR 44 Amount of noise from outside	0.34623	VAR 49 Problems of damp or condensation	0.51940

Component III: (Quality of external environment		Component IV: (Anti-social activity	
VAR 19 General appearance of area	0.37784	VAR 30 Level of vandalism	0.50667
VAR 20 Amount of trees and greenery nearby	0.71453	VAR 31 Security of home from theft	0.37461
VAR 21 Tidiness of streets and surrounding areas	0.55617	VAR 33 Nuisance from roving dogs	0.65931
VAR 22 Amount of smoke and dust in air	0.52060	VAR 36 Reputation of area	0.36740
VAR 51 View from living room	0.41253		

Component V: (Neighbours)		Component VI: (Access to public open space	
VAR 24 Your neighbours	0.55515	VAR 11 Access to countryside	0.38574
VAR 43 Amount of noise from neighbours	0.80392	VAR 12 Availability of parks and play areas	0.67207
VAR 45 Privacy from neighbours	0.60843	VAR 18 Car parking facilities	0.40893
		VAR 32 Availability of safe areas for children to play	0.44035

Component VII: (House internal design)		Component VIII: (Standard of public services)	
VAR 38 Number of rooms	0.67059	VAR 25 Rubbish collection service	0.52974
VAR 39 Size and layout of rooms	0.70483	VAR 26 Standard of street lighting	0.58808

Component IX: (Access to private open space)	
VAR 41 Amount of outside space for own use	0.35427
VAR 50 Amount of sunlight you receive	0.88091

Table 5.5 Component structures: neighbourhood analysis

Component I: (Traffic problems)

VAR 16	Noise from traffic	0.879
VAR 15	Amount of traffic on streets	0.863
VAR 17	Risk of traffic accidents	0.762

Component II: (Quality of external environment - cleanliness)

VAR 26	Standard of street lighting	0.608
VAR 25	Rubbish collection service	0.600
VAR 36	Reputation of area	0.546
VAR 21	Tidiness of streets and surrounding areas	0.458
VAR 22	Amount of smoke and dust in air	0.363
VAR 23	Standard of maintenance of communal areas	0.335

Component III: (Access to public open space)

VAR 12	Availability of parks and play areas	0.541
VAR 32	Availability of safe areas for children to play	0.538
VAR 18	Car parking facilities	0.526

Component IV: (Anti-social activity)

VAR 30	Level of vandalism	0.631
VAR 33	Nuisance from roving dogs	0.571
VAR 31	Security of home from theft	0.490

Component V: (Accessibility)

VAR 05	Ease of reaching city centre shops	0.777
VAR 04	Journey time to work	0.499
VAR 10	Distance to entertainments	0.423
VAR 03	Goods and Services available locally	0.310
VAR 14	Availability of health services	0.309

Component VI: (Quality of social contacts)

VAR 09	Distance to friends and relatives	0.568
VAR 24	Your neighbours	0.558

Component VII: (Quality of external environment - greenery)

VAR 19	General appearance of area	0.321
VAR 20	Amount of trees and greenery nearby	0.829

Table 5.6   Component structures: dwelling unit analysis

Component I: (House physical structure)

VAR 42 Standard of building and internal repair	0.809
VAR 40 Outside appearance of house/flat	0.516
VAR 51 View from living room	0.427
VAR 49 Problems of damp or condensation	0.411

Component II: (Access to private open space

VAR 50 Amount of sunlight	0.972
VAR 41 Amount of outside space for own use	0.360

Component III: (Neighbours)

VAR 43 Amount of noise from neighbours	0.747
VAR 45 Privacy from neighbours	0.631

Component IV: (House:internal design

VAR 38 Number of rooms	0.806
VAR 39 Size and layout of rooms	0.544

Component V: (House:running costs)

VAR 48 Cost of heating	0.517
VAR 46 Level of rent	0.431
VAR 47 Efficiency of heating system	0.373

The inclusion of components IV (house: internal design) and V (house: running costs) in the rotated solution was significant, particularly as some writers have suggested that these factors are of little importance within the council housing sector. English (1979), for example, stated that 'two factors which are of relatively little significance in the public sector are price and size of dwelling: rent structures are usually relatively few with only modest variations according to quality, while housing departments are generally only willing to allocate accommodation of the 'correct' size.   The present findings cast doubt on the general applicability of such a conclusion. A common level of council house rent does not alleviate the problem of payment when unemployment is the normal state of most adults (two-thirds of the household heads interviewed were out of work), just as allocation of a 'correct size' house at one point in time is of little practical benefit when family circumstances change due to births or new household formation (overcrowding is a serious problem in Ferguslie Park as Table 5.1 indicates; one sample household, for example, contained eight persons, four of whom were children of pre-school age).

REGRESSION ANALYSES

Having identified the criteria employed by residents and the major components of residential environmental quality a logical next step was to examine the relationship between each component and residents' general evaluations of their neighbourhood and of their dwelling respectively. One solution to the problem of assessing the contribution of each component to overall satisfaction with the neighbourhood and the dwelling is by means of regression analysis since in regression attention is focussed on the dependence of one variable Y on a number of other independent variables. The precise method

adopted was a step-wise regression procedure which computed the sum
of squares which each independent variable and co-variable removed,
after first adjusting for the effect of every other independent variable and co-variable. The step-wise procedure ranked independent
variables according to their ability to reduce the variation in the
dependent variable remaining at each step. Component scores for
each of the 150 respondents on each of the components in the two
principal component analyses carried out with the disaggregated sets
of variables formed the raw data for the independent variables in
the regression. The dependent variables (VAR 01 and VAR 37)
(Table 5.3) comprised each residents' overall assessment of his
neighbourhood and dwelling environments.

Table 5.7 provides summary descriptions of the results of each
of the regression analyses. In terms of neighbourhood satisfaction
four variables included in the regression equation by the F value
of 0.01 explained 41.0 per cent of the variance, while for dwelling
unit satisfaction three variables accounted for 34.0 per cent. Of
greater importance for the objectives of the present study, however,
was the order in which the variables entered the equation. The
largest contribution to neighbourhood satisfaction was made by the
component related to 'quality of social contacts'(Table 5.5). This
variable accounted for 27 per cent of the variance and served to
underline the importance of inter-personal relations in creating
and maintaining a satisfactory living environment. Next in importance was the component identified with 'anti-social activity' which
focussed on the incidence of vandalism, housebreaking and nuisance
from roving dogs. Ranked third in terms of its contribution to
neighbourhood satisfaction was component II (Table 5.5) which was
highly correlated with six variables all related to the 'cleanliness
of the physical environment'. This was complemented by the final
significant variable to enter the equation (Component VII) which
provided a measure of the 'greenness of the neighbourhood environment'.

Three components were found to be significantly related to residents' satisfaction with their dwelling. First in importance was
component IV (Table 5.6) which measured the internal design of the
house and referred specifically to the size, layout and number of
rooms available. This was followed into the equation by component
I (Table 5.6) which was a measure of the physical structure of the
dwelling based on a range of criteria such as the standard of building and internal repair, external appearance, view from living
room, and problems of damp or excessive condensation. Finally,
ranked third was an indicator of residents' access to open space, in
the form of parks and safe areas for children to play.

SUMMARY AND CONCLUSION

In terms of the principal objectives of the research, the major components of a satisfactory residential environment were isolated
using a multi-variate analysis of data collected by means of a sample survey of residents in a council housing development. Understanding of the relative importance of each component was gained by
examining the results of principal components and regression analyses
of the data set.

The potential of sample surveys of the type employed here has
not been fully realised by decision-makers. Information gathered in
this way may be employed in the identification of policy priorities;
this is of particular importance in times of public expenditure con-
straint. Concerning housing, for example, action may be targetted
to the most appropriate geographic scale (estate, neighbourhood or
dwelling) as well as focussed onto specific components at each level
(e.g. problems of damp or condensation in houses; or of a vandalised

Table 5.7 Regression analyses: summary statistics

1. Neighbourhood

DIMENSION	MULT.R	R^2	F	SIG F	B	BETA
Quality of Social Contacts	0.5165	0.2668	60.461	0.000	0.92724	0.49343
Anti-social Activity	0.5715	0.3266	11.465	0.001	0.40108	0.21526
Quality of External Environment: Cleanliness	0.6119	0.3745	10.407	0.002	0.38212	0.20642
Quality of External Environment: Greenery	0.6407	0.4105	8.914	0.003	0.33511	0.18923

2. Dwelling Unit

DIMENSION	MULT.R	R^2	F	SIG F	B	BETA
House Internal Design	0.4135	0.1710	33.989	0.000	0.52687	0.39395
House Physical Structure	0.5556	0.3087	29.006	0.000	0.47621	0.36427
Access to Private Open Space	0.5788	0.3350	5.782	0.017	0.18358	0.16246

external environment) in order to maximise the benefits for residents.

Finally, the evidence from the present investigation strongly suggests that, if real improvements in the quality of life for council house residents are to be achieved, local planning authorities with a responsibility for housing must make greater use of the 'subjective' approach and incorporate residents' revealed preferences in any measure of residential quality. The type of methodology described represents a valuable complement to the traditional measures of residential environmental quality.

REFERENCES

Abrams, M. 1972. Subjective social indicators. *Social Trends,* 4.

Andrews, F.M. and Withey, S.B. 1976. *Social Indicators of Well Being: Americans Perceptions of Life Quality.* (New York).

Burisch, M. 1979. Subjective versus normative evaluation of housing quality. *Journal of Consumer Policy,* 3, 59-70.

Campbell, A. and Converse, P.E. 1972. *The Human Meaning of Social Change.* (New York).

Duncan, T.L.C. 1971. Measuring Housing Quality: a study of methods. *C.U.R.S. University of Birmingham Occasional Paper No. 20.*

English, J. 1976. Housing allocation and a deprived Scottish estate. *Urban Studies,* 13, 319-323.

English, J. 1979. Access and deprivation in local authority housing, in *Urban Deprivation and the Inner City,* C. Jones (ed), (Croom Helm, London), 113-135.

Francescato, G. 1980. The quality of the residential environment: European housing after WW2, in *Western European Cities in Crisis,* M.C. Romanos (ed), (Heath, Lexington), 31-46.

Fried, M. and Gleicher, P. 1961. Some sources of residential satisfaction in an urban area. *Journal of the American Institute of Planners,* 27.

Gans, H.J. 1967. Planning and city planning for mental health, in *Taming Metropolis,* H.W. Eldredge (ed), (New York).

Hall, J. 1976. Subjective measures of quality of life in Britain 1971-1975: some developments and trends. *Social Trends,* 7, 47-60.

Harman, H. 1960. *Modern Factor Analysis.* (Chicago).

Hoinville, G. 1971. Evaluating community preferences. *Environment and Planning,* 3, 35-50.

Johnston, R.J. 1978. *Multivariate Statistical Analysis in Geography.* (Longman, London).

Marans, R.W. and Rodgers, W.L. 1974. Toward an understanding of community satisfaction, in *Metropolitan America: Papers on the state of knowledge,* A. Hawley and V. Rock (eds), (National Acad. of Sciences, Washington D.C.).

Merton, R.K. 1968. *Social Theory and Social Structure.* (New York).

Michelson, W. 1977. *Environmental Choice, Human Behaviour and Residential Satisfaction.* (Oxford Univ. Press).

Rent, G.S. and Rent, C.S. 1978. Low income housing: factors related to residential satisfaction. *Environment and Behaviour,* 10(4), 459-488.

Sanoff, H. and Sawhney, M. 1972. Residential desirability: a study of user attitudes towards their residential environment, in *Environmental Design: Research and Practice,* W.J. Mitchell (ed), EDRA 3, U.C.L.A. 13/8/1 - 13/8/10. (Univ. of California Press).

Tauber, G. and Levin, J. 1971. Public housing as neighbourhood: the effect of local and non-local participation. *Social Science Quarterly,* 52, 534-42.

Chapter 6

Devising a Local Strategy for

a Deprived Housing Area: Ferguslie Park

Alex Robertson

INTRODUCTION

Ferguslie Park has been described as one of the most deprived housing estates in Scotland. This paper describes some of its problems and gives details of two different attempts to devise local strategies.

PROFILE OF RENFREW DISTRICT

Like the other 52 second tier local authorities in Scotland, Renfrew District was formed in 1975, and brought together the large burgh of Paisley, three small burghs, and a sizeable part of Renfrewshire. It is situated on the western edge of Glasgow and with a population of just over 200 000 is comparable in size to Dundee or Aberdeen. The product of a penny rate produces £540 000 for the District Council - considerably less than was the case just four years ago. This can largely be attributed to the economic recession, not least of all the closedown of the Talbot car plant at Linwood. The main function of the authority is housing, and there are just under 40 000 Council houses within the District's boundaries. This represents 51 per cent of the total housing stock. Since Ferguslie Park has 2500 houses (almost entirely owned by the Council) it makes up a significant part of the public sector housing stock in the District.

Development of Ferguslie Park, 1925-65

Ferguslie Park is a large local authority housing scheme built mainly under the slum clearance legislation of the 1930s, located on the edge of Paisley urban area, surrounded on three sides by railways and motorways with only one major access road (see Fig. 5.2). Although there are small areas of well maintained housing, a general impression of neglect is conveyed in many parts of the scheme where tenemental buildings have fallen into disrepair. In April 1982, out of the original 3536 Council houses in Ferguslie Park, about 380 were lying empty and 950 had been demolished. There are persistent problems of vandalism and litter, no equipped parks and only a few swings and goalposts. The wide streets, sometimes strewn with broken glass and other debris, the boarded up tenements and the muddy open spaces present a bleak and dismal picture. There are two small clusters of shops, defended by shutters or iron grilles when closed, and two or three general stores.

Ferguslie Park, like most stigmatised areas, is often regarded as a homogeneous area. Yet both in terms of its physical and social characteristics it is highly diverse. It was not built in a single phase, but over a 40 year period stretching from 1925. Most of it was built during the 1930s and 1940s for slum clearance rehousing and so it was established as a deprived and stigmatised area. The unpopularity was exacerbated by the high proportion of tenements compared with other schemes. Once established the unpopularity meant that waiting times for houses were relatively short so that it has been mainly applicants who were constrained to obtain accommodation quickly who accepted houses in Ferguslie Park. Many of those people were suffering social stress and sharing accommodation because of financial difficulties or domestic crises. Therefore they tend, for example, to be unemployed, have low incomes or be single parents. In short, poor housing and environmental conditions, unpopularity, difficulty in letting houses and deprivation tend to go together. (Paisley CDP 1976). It was the building of the most recent group of houses in Ferguslie Park - 224 in all - in 1965, together with an active burgh-wide local authority building programme in the late 1960s that led to the emergence of a local surplus in 1968. That feature, together with a policy of allocating families with problems, over a period of years to Ferguslie Park, led to a progressive de-population of the estate.

Demolition and social patterns

The de-population in turn led to demolition after 1970 and has continued unabated since. Hence a population of 13 500 has fallen to an estimated 8000 today and 950 houses have been demolished in the process. Over the past 12 years there have been about 80 houses demolished every year. Significantly enough this trend has shown no sign of slowing down. An exercise recently carried out by the District Council has demonstrated that over the past 20 months, the de-population and demolition trends have been almost identical to the pattern over the longer period. Despite this massive demolition, we always appear to be left with about 300 empty houses. These are not only empty and boarded up, but in most instances require considerable capital resources to make them lettable. In many cases this amounts to £3-4000 per house. The level of empty houses is particularly severe just now, due principally to an unusually hard winter. At April, 1982, there were 380 empty houses on the estate. The combined effects of serious water damage to houses, through burst pipes, requiring tenants to be rehoused, and the higher than usual abscondency rate produced an estimated 80 or 90 additional empty houses since December, 1981. Once houses have been empty for some time, the effects of weather, vandalism and the stigmatisation of the scheme make it extremely hard to get them back into the housing stock.

It is worth noting that while Ferguslie Park has 14 per cent of its houses empty, the District as a whole has only a two per cent vacancy rate. Or expressed another way, it has six per cent of the District's houses, but 40 per cent of its empty property. Quite clearly, the difficult-to-let houses problem in Renfrew District is a highly concentrated one. Returning to the point about Ferguslie Park's lack of homogeneity, however, the empty houses are far from being evenly spread throughout the estate. A glance at Table 6.1 shows that some areas are hardly affected by empty houses at all. On the other hand, areas such as Candren (Area 8) and Ferguslie Park Crescent (Area 7) can have one house in five or even one house in three vacant.

The quality of life and human welfare for those tenants remaining in such areas obviously leaves much to be desired. When one appreciates that the areas having most empty and greatest *physical*

66

Table 6.1   Housing stock in Ferguslie Park

		Total houses	Empty at March, 1982
Area 1	(Crudens)	224	14 (6%)
2	(Westmarch)	240	7 (3%)
3	(Tannahill)	442	10 (2%)
4	(Blackstoun)	160	1 (1%)
5	(Bankfoot/Darkwood)	338	39 (11%)
6	(Westburn)	249	27 (11%)
7	(Dalskieth/Ferguslie Park Crescent)	457	200 (40%)
8	(Candren)	318	66 (20%)
9	(Belltrees)	130	15 (14%)
	TOTAL	2558	379 (14%)

deterioration correspond very closely with those of greatest *social* stress, the situation becomes even more severe. This fact has been established from numerous discussions with social workers in the local Area Office. Living within a very bleak physical environment, therefore, we have small concentrations of people who are amongst the most socially and economically deprived of any in Strathclyde Region. Irrespective of which social indicators are chosen - physical and mental handicap, unemployment, single parent families, large families, low incomes - Ferguslie Park consistently emerges as a relatively poor area.

AREA BASED APPROACHES TO DEPRIVATION IN THE U.K.

Having sketched profiles of Renfrew District and Ferguslie Park, there is a need to provide some background information on area based approaches to urban deprivation in the United Kingdom. More detailed discussion of this aspect is, however, available in the papers given by M. Danson and K. Yates (chapters 3 and 4).
    In the mid and late 1960s, conventional wisdom began to express 'regret' that certain council housing estates built between the wars or immediately after the war had been designed with insufficient community facilities and a surfeit of tenemental buildings. Doubts were also expressed about certain housing management policies. This massive national problem, however, was not given official recognition in Scotland until after the publication of the SHAC Report in 1970. This report, along with others which followed, explained the neglected role of preventive policies (Local Government Unit, Paisley, 1981). This was also the period when participation and community involvement became fashionable in Britain. Moreover, national commitments to the problems of poverty and deprivation - such as the Urban Programme and the Community Development Projects - were set up. (Ferguslie Park CDP was one of 12 throughout the UK). Both of these were established by the Wilson government in 1968, but did not get into full swing until a few years later.
    It was this new climate that led some Scottish local authorities in the early 1970s to embark on a variety of attacks on the problems of estates whose distinguishing feature was increasingly seen as their stigmatisation. Generally, these national and local programmes attempted to achieve four relatively new objectives. These were:

a) positive discrimination

b) co-ordination of activities

c) local participation

d) critical review of departmental policies

Towards the end of this paper, I will return to these four objectives and assess their success with respect to the Ferguslie Park Strategy.

ADMINISTRATIVE STRUCTURES IN RENFREW DISTRICT

Shortly after re-organisation, and in line with certain other Scottish local authorities, Renfrew District Council devised various administrative structures to tackle its problems of urban deprivation. But since the initial structure was developed various changes have been made in response to changing circumstances and priorities. By September, 1976 the Council had established the following:

a) a Deprived Areas Sub Committee of the Policy and Resources Committee

b) a Ferguslie Park Project Team of officials

c) a Working Party of senior officials to prepare a comprehensive plan for Deprived Areas and Areas at Risk.

Initially, these structures worked fairly well, but on coming to power in May, 1980, the Labour Group on the Council decided to make the previous Deprived Areas Sub Committee a full standing Committee of the authority and called it the Community Development Committee. This development was fairly significant since it not only gave the Committee Convener more clout than her predecessor, but reflected a greater commitment to the deprived areas. This administrative change was followed in August, 1980 by the appointment of a Co-ordinator and an Assistant Co-ordinator - the first officials employed by the Council who were concerned full-time with deprivation issues.

Why have a local strategy at all?

Since local authorities already produce large numbers of reports, plans and strategies, it is reasonable to ask if it is necessary to have yet another kind of plan - this time for a deprived area. In the seven years since reorganisation, Scottish local authorities have produced Regional Reports, Structure Plans, Housing Plans, Finance Plans, Local Plans, Local Subject Plans and a host of other *ad hoc* reports. Surely it is not necessary to devise a special strategy for deprived areas or one particular deprived area? Yet it can be argued strongly that the problems of places like Ferguslie Park are significantly large enough and sufficiently different enough from the general problems of the Districts within which they are located that the absence of a local strategy greatly increases the likelihood of repeating the expensive mistakes of the past. The word 'expensive' is used not only in terms of financial losses such as the demolition of houses, or the rehabilitation of houses which fail to attract new tenants. It is also used in terms of the human misery which is the necessary concomitant of the failure to solve or ameliorate the problems. One of the recurring features of areas such as Ferguslie Park is the lack of co-ordination among the various departments and agencies which have the resources and skills to tackle the enormous, fundamental problems. Without a local strategy which can be agreed upon by the various parties (including the local community itself) it is almost impossible to achieve the necessary co-ordination: and without co-ordination each agency will continue to operate in an isolated manner without the mutual support and understanding of other agencies tackling different aspects of the same problems.

THE FIRST STRATEGY FOR FERGUSLIE PARK, 1977-80

The first attempt at a comprehensive Strategy was produced between 1977 and 1979. In the latter year the District Council approved a programme for the modernisation of Ferguslie Park. That programme envisaged full modernisation and environmental improvement of 2354 houses together with some short term wind and watertight repairs and rehabilitation of vacant houses. Ninty six houses were to be demolished. The strategy envisaged 17 phases of modernisation over 14 years, but the first two years were to be devoted largely to a pilot scheme involving only 44 houses. It would have been several years before work started on many of the poorest and most vulnerable houses. The total cost to Renfrew District Council, estimated at November, 1978 prices, was £19.4 million suggesting an average annual cost of £1.4 million, although something like £1.8 million was scheduled to be spent in each of the middle years of the programme. For their part, the Regional Council always expressed reservations about the practicability and equity of the Strategy. In late 1980, two factors caused the District Council to decide to review this programme:

a) the effect of government expenditure policies on the ability of the District Council to carry out its Housing Capital expenditure programme; and

b) the deteriorating condition of many properties in the area. At that time there were 300 houses vacant and many of these were considered by the Housing Department to be unlettable.

Thus, a combination of changes in Central Government policy, a rise in the unit expenditure levels to £15 000 - £19 000 for full modernisation of the worst of the housing stock, and a worsening of the empty house situation, led to the abandonment of the first Ferguslie Park Strategy. If the original Strategy had prevailed, then by the time the most vulnerable areas had been due to be modernised, (late 1980s at the earliest, but probably later because of cutbacks) their future would have been in doubt due to the likely level of empty houses and possible demolitions.

THE SECOND STRATEGY FOR FERGUSLIE PARK, 1981-82

As a result, a new improvement Strategy was produced by the District Council's Deprivation Policy Group in January, 1981. It was approved by the full Council in August, 1981 and still remains Council policy.

i) The Strategy clearly states that all proposals for Ferguslie Park should be seen within the context of housing need for the District as a whole. It would be pointless for example, to recommend major demolition of houses in Ferguslie Park if it is later discovered that the District Council cannot afford to lose that stock. In short, the proposals should be seen as an integral part of the Housing Plan.

ii) This led directly to the proposal that demolition should be kept to a minimum, but it was accepted that some demolition of the worst properties (then estimated, at about 80) would be inevitable. This recommendation was devised partly to ensure that most resources earmarked for Ferguslie Park went into positive improvement of the scheme. The precise number of demolitions will depend on changing circumstances but continuous monitoring will be undertaken.

iii) Thirdly, it is not merely a plan for physical improvement, but one of community development with a more comprehensive set of policies.

iv) The Strategy involves both the District and Regional Councils and has the agreement of the community. In this context, the Strategy received the support of the Regional Council in October, 1981 and a number of meetings have been held with various community groups from the estate.

v) Attention (including modernisation) should be focussed on Areas 5-9 (see Table 6.1) - i.e. the areas of greatest physical and social problems.

vi) Rather than full modernisation, it is now policy to spend less per house and therefore cover a wider area. Failure to adopt this policy would have implied a greater number of demolitions in the short term. The first area to be treated in this way is Belltrees, Area 9, and the 130 houses are currently receiving new kitchens and bathrooms as well as being rewired and insulated. Unit costs are about £3400. Tenant participation is clearly a key part of this process.

vii) In the case of 22 industrialised houses at Barochan Crescent, within the most vulnerable part of the estate, however, full modernisation is going ahead since the only alternative for these particular houses was demolition. Moreover, the house type is popular and there is a good degree of stability in this small enclave due to the low number of transfer requests.

viii) It was hoped that the combination of the modernisation work carried out in Belltrees and Barochan Crescent together with future work carried out in adjacent areas would result in an expansion of the good areas and a corresponding contraction of the poor areas.

ix) At the same time, it is accepted by the Council that attention will still be given to rehabilitating and letting empty houses so as to make this particular problem more manageable. But the emphasis was expected to shift towards improving houses with sitting tenants as the Strategy proceeded.

x) Another small, though significant element in the Strategy is the application of wind and watertight treatment to house exteriors in advance of the partial internal modernisation mentioned at (vi) above.

Due to the fact that the District Council only receives its Housing Capital Allocation from Scottish Office for one year at a time, few detailed proposals were made beyond financial years 1981/82 and 1982/83. In any case, it was acknowledged that flexibility should be a keynote of the Strategy and there would be a need to closely monitor changing circumstances and respond to these in terms of detailed implementation. The capital sums contained for the Ferguslie Park Strategy as a result of several Council decisions are shown in Table 6.2.

Table 6.2 Capital sums for the Ferguslie Park Strategy

	1981/82	1982/83
(a) Construction of railway wall	£ 35 000	-
(b) Rehabilitation of empty houses	260 000	£200 000
(c) Wind/Watertight repairs	30 000	30 000
(d) Planned Demolition	45 000	-
(e) Limited modernisation of Belltrees (130 houses)	125 000	275 000
(f) Full modernisation of 22 BISF houses at Barochan Crescent	150 000	180 000
TOTAL	£645 000	£685 000

In addition to the key elements of the Strategy mentioned above, there are a number of other matters which have to be investigated. Much of this investigative work is already underway and as policy decisions are taken on each matter the Strategy will slowly evolve and develop. The matters under investigation include:

a) discussions with private developers to explore the provision of new private houses in gap sites or the possible rehabilitation of private housing stock;

b) consideration of the possible 'homesteading' of houses deemed to be unlettable along similar lines to the Easterhouse project;

c) investigation on the provision of an Area Centre to provide a 'one door' approach for most local authority services - Social Work; Housing; Technical Services and Education. Hopefully, this would make services more accessible, facilitate corporate action at a fieldwork level and encourage community participation;

d) the advertising for new tenants who have a local connection in cases of difficult-to-let housing.

In brief, the Strategy's aims can be summarised as attempting to make Ferguslie Park a more attractive place in which to live; to concentrate physical improvements in the areas of greatest physical and social stress; to reduce the number of empty houses; and to work closely with the Regional Council and local people. :

ASSESSMENT

This paper has tended to concentrate upon the physical dimensions of the improvement Strategy. This is not to indicate that the Council believes that the social and economic dimensions are less important in Ferguslie Park. However, there are two very good reasons why the Strategy approved by the Council emphasises the physical aspects. In the first place, the Council's main function is housing, while social and economic matters tend to be the responsibility of either Central Government agencies or the Regional Council. In the second place, the key issue in Ferguslie Park is housing - irrespective of how many social workers, teachers and policemen are locally employed, if the housing stock remains in a vulnerable condition then many of the other social policies will be to little avail.

Returning now to the four objectives already mentioned above it is worth looking at each in turn to measure its success with respect to the Ferguslie Park Strategy.

Taking positive discrimination first, it is a fact that at no time in the life of the authority, unlike Strathclyde Regional Council, has Renfrew District ever had an explicit policy of positive discrimination towards Ferguslie Park or any other of its deprived areas. Yet this is not to say that positive discrimination has not been practised, for in several important instances it has. Specifically, looking at the Council's housing capital programmes for 1981-82 and 1982-83, Ferguslie Park has received some 11 or 12 per cent of the budget although it has only six per cent of the houses. Although this constitutes clear positive discrimination, it is a matter for debate whether or not these considerable resources are sufficient for the magnitude of the problem. But given the other problems and priorities of the authority, for example, Housing Action Areas, sheltered housing and other special needs, and rewiring programmes, it is unlikely that the percentages could be increased without the capital allocation from Scottish Office being increased. Capital allocations, in turn, do not depend upon social need but upon the level of rents and the cash receipts received from Council house sales.

Much room for improvement in terms of the co-ordination of services still remains. However, steady improvements are being made in respect of this objective. The District's Deprivation Policy Group and the Region's Divisional Deprivation Group provide valuable forums for the co-ordination of activities. At the fieldwork and implementation level, the establishment of an Area Centre should do much to encourage local authority workers from different disciplines to discuss common problems and give mutual support.

According to community workers and tenants in Ferguslie Park, local participation is probably better just now than it has been for some considerable time. This should not signal complacency, because there are still times when participation between the service departments and the tenants is conspicuous by its absence. Nevertheless, the progress made so far should provide a good basis for further developing links with a number of healthy Tenants Associations in the area. Modernisation proposals and discussions on community facilities provide the sort of issues where tenants can and do get involved.

Finally, a critical review of departmental policies is the objective where most difficulties arise. Questions of accountability, precedent and attitudes make it extremely difficult to implement changes. Yet certain encouraging signs are apparent on the horizon. The Social Work Department's recent *Social Needs and Social Work Resources* review is a good example of progress. Similarly, the District Council is currently having wide discussions on how services are provided in its deprived areas. Over a period of years, these discussions will doubtless assist in making appropriate changes to service delivery in Ferguslie Park and elsewhere.

REFERENCES

Gilbert, J. and Rosenburgh, L. 1980. *Housing Investment Strategies for difficult to let Public Sector Housing Estates.* (Scottish Development Department).

Local Government Unit, Paisley. *Difficult to let Housing.* (Unpublished Paper, Paisley College).

National C.D.P. 1976. *Whatever happened to Council Housing.*

Paisley C.D.P. 1977. *A Profile of Ferguslie Park.*

Paisley C.D.P. 1977. *Social Work in the Primary School.*

Renfrew District Council, 1979. *Housing Plan, 1980-85.* Contains the first Strategy for Ferguslie Park.

Renfrew District Council, 1981. *A Physical Improvement Strategy for Ferguslie Park.*

Shelter, Scotland, 1981. *Dead End Street.*

Strathclyde Regional Council, 1981. *Social Needs and Social Work Resources in Renfrew Division.*

Chapter 7

Environmental Quality in Stirling

Ian Moffatt

INTRODUCTION

The improvement of environmental quality cannot be separated from the improvement of conditions under which people have to work and live. In Scotland it has been estimated that 3.5 million people (67.3 per cent) work and live in urban areas with a minimum population threshold set at 10 000 (Best, 1976). Given this distribution of population, it would be expected that numerous studies into environmental quality would have adopted an urban focus. Unfortunately, there have been very few studies which have focused upon environmental quality in British urban areas. Indeed the absence of studies of urban environmental quality in Scotland is surprising given the large number of people living in Scottish towns and cities.

This paper attempts to initiate research into environmental quality in Scottish urban areas by reporting upon a preliminary survey undertaken in the burgh of Stirling. In the following section, the pattern of environmental quality in Stirling is described, using both objective and subjective data. Next, on the basis of this survey and drawing upon the limited literature concerned with environmental quality in western cities, a conceptual model is presented as a focus for future research. Finally, the results of this preliminary survey are discussed briefly within the context of planning for environmental quality and human welfare in urban areas.

ENVIRONMENTAL QUALITY IN STIRLING

Definitions and the setting

It is exceedingly difficult to define the term 'environmental quality' (Huebner and Paul, 1979). Most urban researchers would, however, agree that environmental quality is closely associated with the various levels of pollution in an area (Wood et al., 1974; Wood, 1979). According to Kapp, the quality of the urban environment goes far beyond air and water pollution and includes, 'excessive noise, urban congestion, long hours spent in travel to and from work in metropolitan areas under chaotic traffic conditions marked by long delays and high accident rates, the progressive absorption of free space and open landscapes, increasing specialisation and monotony of work in some; and hectic performance requirements in other professions'. (Kapp, 1974, 102). Unfortunately, data for including these various attributes of environmental quality are not readily available and hence individual researchers have had to design their own definitions and measures of environmental quality. (Perloff, 1969).

In Britain detailed quantitative studies into environmental quality in urban areas have been hampered by the lack of appropriate statistical information. One of the most comprehensive studies into urban environmental pollution has been undertaken in greater Manchester (Wood et al., 1974). Whilst the data base was not exhaustive it was possible to construct a composite pollution index for each of the seventy-one local authority areas which made up the greater Manchester conurbation. This index included concentration of smoke and sulphur dioxide as indicators of air pollution, the areal extent of spoil heaps for land pollution, traffic density as a crude measure of noise pollution and the level of biochemical oxygen demand for water quality in the rivers and canals running through Manchester. The spatial pattern of the composite pollution index was then compared with the socio-economic groups in the conurbation. It was demonstrated that there was a statistically significant high correlation between the level of atmospheric pollution, as measured by the smoke concentration in the summer of 1966, and the socio-economic distribution of population in greater Manchester. Furthermore, the study revealed that all the pollutants have their greatest environmental effect upon certain of the less affluent sections of the population of greater Manchester (Wood et al., 1974).

In order to understand the differential impact that environmental pollution has upon the inhabitants of an urban area, it is necessary first of all to discuss the actual pattern of land use; in this case of Stirling. Although Stirling has a medieval nucleus including a castle, wall, and church, the burgh did not expand physically until after the railway arrived in 1848. By 1851 the population of Stirling had reached 10 006 when much of the area between the medieval nucleus and the railway in the east had been developed. According to Gordon, urban development southwards almost linked Stirling with the village of St. Ninians and 'this phase of growth transformed the predominantly north-west south-east alignment of the medieval burgh into the north-south arrangement of the nineteenth and twentieth century' (Gordon, 1974).

The physical expansion of the town was also accompanied by social and residential differentiation throughout the nineteenth and twentieth centuries. Between 1850 and 1901, for example, a Victorian villa suburb was built between the old medieval nucleus and the Crown land of King's Park. This development was, and still is, a predominantly middle-class area of Stirling. In the east of the burgh a small working class development grew up around Nelson Place, Burghmuir and Colquhoun Street, whilst a set of two-storey tenements and small terraced houses were concentrated in Riverside between 1881 and 1921.

As in many British towns and cities, local authority housing assumed an important role in the creation of the residential areas for predominantly working class people. The largest inter-war development occurred at Raploch located between the castle and the River Forth; local authority housing estates also springing up in the vicinity of St. Ninians. More recently a private housing development in the Torbrex area has emerged. The general pattern of the growth and residential differentiation of Stirling is shown in Figure 7.1.

An objective survey

As in the greater Manchester study, four objective indicators of environmental pollution were employed in the preliminary survey of Stirling. The first two indicators included the annual domestic sulphur dioxide and smoke emissions measured by the local authority

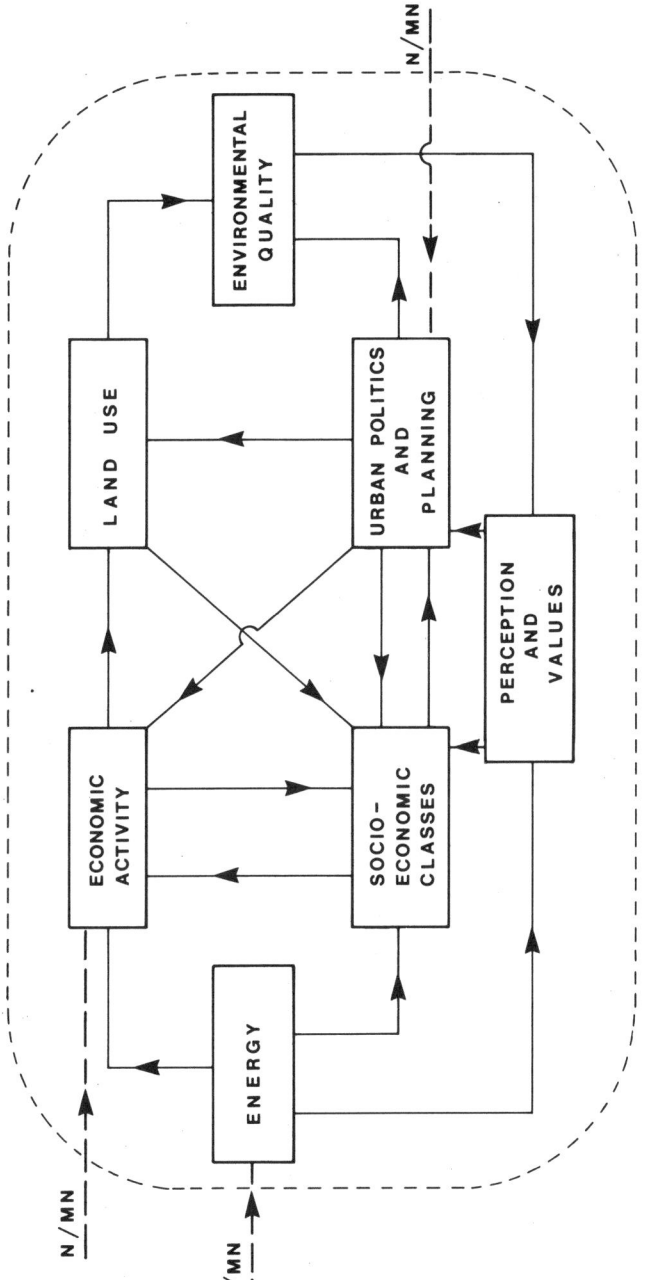

Figure 7.1 A transect showing variations in Stirling's environment

- - - - - System boundary.

──► Exogenous influences National and Multi-National.

──► Interdependencies.

in thousands of kilograms over the period July, 1973 to March, 1977 (Keddie *et al.*, 1978). The third indicator used the biochemical oxygen demand (BOD) for the River Forth running through the burgh and measured in mg/1. The BOD levels have been monitored by the River Forth Purification Board over the summer months for fifteen years (1960-1975) but, despite improvements in the water quality, the 1977 annual report noted that, 'between Stirling and Alloa Inch the estuary is uniformly poor quality... large numbers of faecal coliform associated with the large input of industrial and domestic wastes to the area' (River Forth Purification Board, 1977). The fourth indicator of environmental quality used in this study was the amount of derelict land in the burgh based on urban field work (Table 7.1).

As the indicators of environmental pollution are measured in different units each indicator was standardized in a scale ranging from 0 to 100, the lower figure representing a better quality of the environment. The standardized scores for each indicator were then summed and the mean value was plotted on a grid square lattice super- imposed on the base map. Each grid square represented one quarter hectare (Figure 7.2). The highest concentrations of environmental pollution, as recorded by this pollution index, occur in the north of Stirling around the bridges which cross the River Forth. This area is characterized by some industry, including a meat factory, and derelict land adjacent to the railway line. In addition, the smoke and sulphur dioxide levels are quite high. To the immediate west and east of the badly polluted area the Raploch area and the western region of Riverside suffer from relatively high levels of pollution ranging from 41 to 80 in the index; the actual amount of smoke and sulphur dioxide being 100 000 and 32 000 kg repectively. Clearly, the predominantly working class areas of Raploch and, to a lesser extent, Riverside, both have a poor environment.

Table 7.1 Objective assessment of environmental pollution

FACTOR	ELEMENT	MEASURE
AIR POLLUTANT	Sulphur Dioxide SO_2	000 kg/yr
AIR POLLUTANT	Smoke Particulates	000 kg/yr
WATER POLLUTANT	Biochemical Oxygen Demand (BOD)	mg/1
LAND POLLUTANT	Derelict Land	% total land use/.25 ha.

The bulk of Stirling does enjoy a reasonable standard of envir- onmental quality. The town centre, the new housing estates adjacent to Burghmuir and the urban development stretching south to St. Ninians are in the second top category for environmental pollution. The areas of the finest environmental quality, however, are located at the urban-rural fringe and include the modern estates at Torbrex and Broomridge as well as the Victorian villa area adjacent to Kings Park.

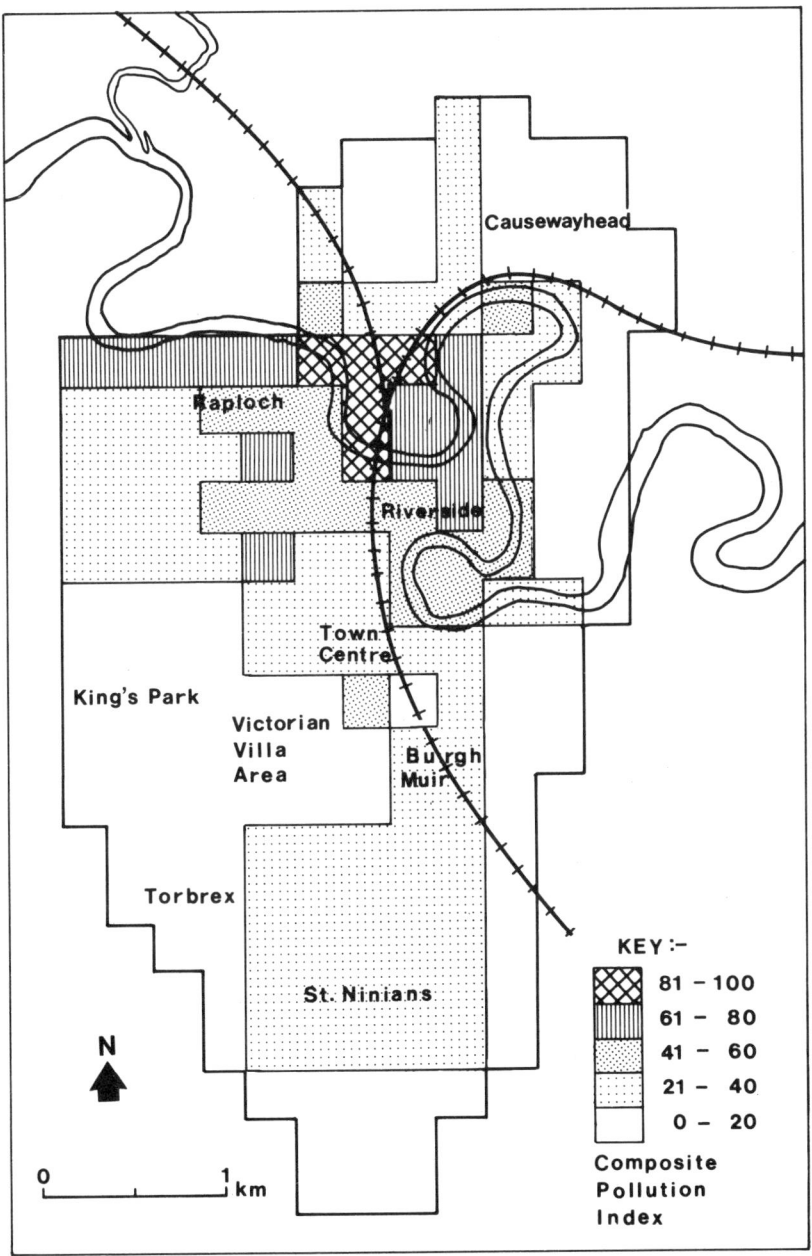

Causewayhead

Raploch

Riverside

Town Centre

King's Park

Victorian Villa Area

Burgh Muir

Torbrex

St. Ninians

N

KEY :-

	81 – 100
	61 – 80
	41 – 60
	21 – 40
	0 – 20

Composite Pollution Index

0 ⊢———⊣ 1 km

Figure 7.2 Objective environmental quality in Stirling

A subjective survey

Whilst it would be desirable to have a more comprehensive objective data set for this survey, several researchers stress that subjective indicators of environmental quality are also important (Coppock and Wilson, 1974; Pacione, 1980). The second method used to evaluate environmental quality within the burgh of Stirling was initially designed by Nottinghamshire County Planning Department and has been used by Dundee University undergraduates in their study of Sheffield (Knox, 1976). In this study several groups of environmental science undergraduates at the University of Stirling took part in the subjective survey. As in the Sheffield survey, a stratified sample of fifty sites was chosen in a radial grid divided into ten equally spaced radii centred on the civic building located in the Corn Exchange. At each site, penalty points were awarded on the basis of four distinctive attributes of the built environment, namely: appearance, access, amenity and provision (Table 7.2). As in the objective survey, the lower the value of the total score at each site the 'better' the quality of the environment.

Table 7.2   Subjective assessment of environmental quality

FACTOR	ELEMENT	WEIGHTING
APPEARANCE	1. Non-conforming use	9
	2. Landscape visual quality	7
	3. Townscape visual quality	5
	4. Appearance of garden/yards	2
	5. Appearance of traffic	3
	sub-total	26
ACCESS	1. To primary school	7
	2. To other urban facilities	6
	3. To children's playground	6
	4. To park/public open space	5
	5. To public transport	5
	sub-total	29
AMENITY	1. Traffic	11
	2. Noise	9
	3. Air pollution	8
	4. Microclimate	4
	sub-total	32
PROVISION	1. Garaging/parking	6
	2. Garden	4
	3. Neighbourhood facilities	3
	sub-total	13
	TOTAL	100

after Knox 1976.

The overall geographical pattern of environmental quality which emerges from this subjective study of Stirling is given in Figure 7.3. As in the objective survey the worst area of environmental quality is located in the west of the Raploch area. The town centre stretching from Cowane Street in the north to the Burghmuir round-about in the south-east is associated with areas of urban decay adjacent to the industrial estate at Burghmuir road. Unlike the objective survey, the Riverside region has quite a reasonable subjective environmental quality. In contrast to Raploch the Riverside area is better provided for by services but does not enjoy easy access to the town centre due, in part, to the main railway line cutting through the eastern section of the town. Again, like the objective study of Stirling, the quality of the environment improves as the urban-rural fringe is approached. In particular the new housing estate at Torbrex and the Victorian villa suburbs of Stirling located in the south-west of the town are areas of highest environmental quality.

Although the two maps of environmental quality are similar in appearance insofar as the worst area of environmental quality is in the north of the town, and the best environmental quality is located in King's Park area, the two distributions are not statistically associated. A Spearman's rank correlation test demonstrated that the rankings of environmental quality on the two maps are independent of one another despite the superficial similarity of the geographical patterns. There was, however, a statistically significant positive correlation between the objective distribution of environmental quality and the socio-economic groupings in the town. Spearman's rank correlation coefficient has a value of $r_s = 0.83$ which was significant at $p = 0.05$. This result supports Wood's earlier study of the distribution of smoke pollution and socio-economic areas in greater Manchester (Wood *et al.*, 1974).

A MODEL OF ENVIRONMENTAL QUALITY

It is clear that any attempt to discuss environmental quality and human welfare in an urban context cannot ignore the interactions of socio-political and bio-physical systems of interest. Unfortunately, the causal analysis of such complex systems is still poorly understood and, as Kapp notes, 'we still lack such a theory and/or science which is capable of elucidating the model and outcome of the complex interaction of several systems' (Kapp, 1974). Nevertheless, it is possible to propose a tentative conceptual model of environmental quality in an urban area to show the interdependencies between socio-political and bio-physical systems (Figure 7.4).

The model consists of seven sub-systems each of which could be disaggregated to provide a more detailed explanation of the processes underlying the pattern of environmental quality in urban areas. At present, however, the model can be described in an aggregate manner to indicate the types of interdependencies in the city conceived of as an environmental system (Douglas, 1981).

At the heart of any city is the supply of energy which is essential for the functioning of a city. Urban energy budgets are very poorly documented with the exception of detailed studies of Hong Kong and Sydney, Australia. Kalma and Newcombe's study demonstrated that spatio-temporal variations in energy use are dependent upon climatic factors and cultural variations in the demographic composition of urban population (Kalma and Newcombe, 1976). One of the obvious manifestations of energy use in the city is the immediate impact on the urban climate as well as on the levels of smoke and sulphur dioxide as noted above. Therefore, it would be possible to monitor some aspects of energy use in British cities in terms of both the inputs and outputs of this sub-system.

81

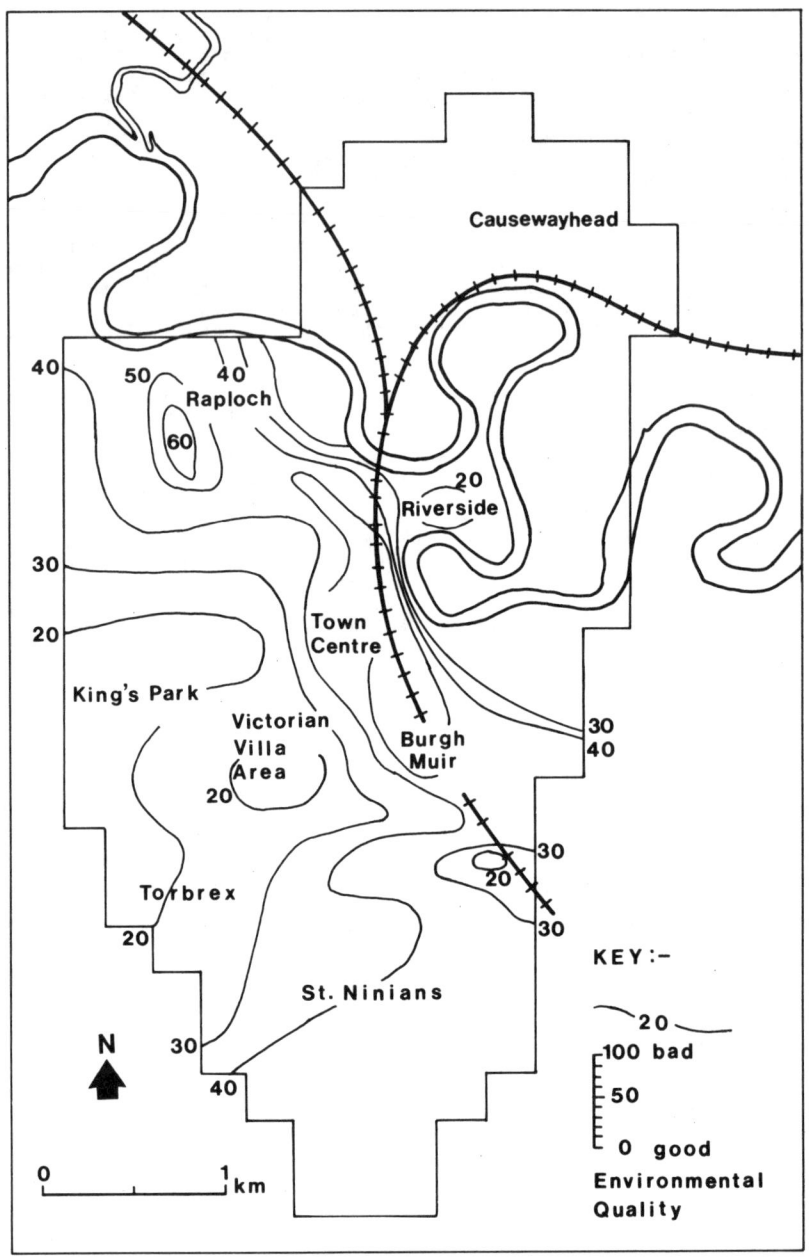

Figure 7.3   Subjective environmental quality in Stirling

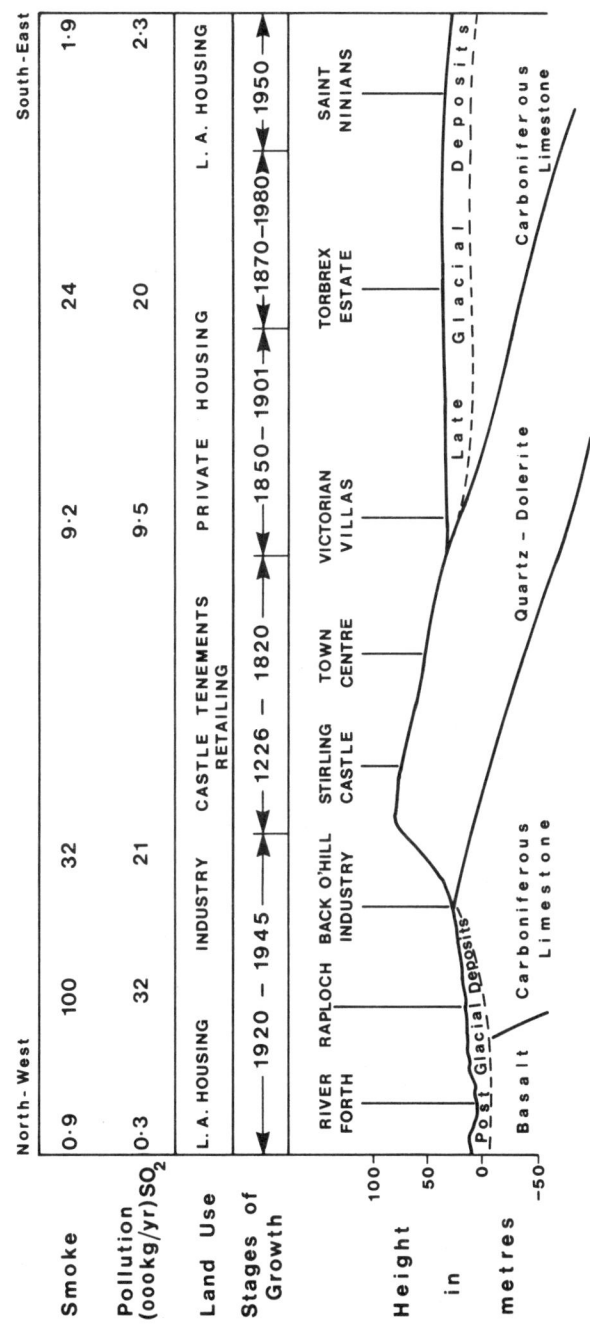

Figure 7.4 Environmental quality in an urban area

The demographic sub-system could be disaggregated by socio-economic and age groups so that the composition of the inhabitants could be finely modelled. Again, the study of environmental quality in Stirling has shown that different sections of the urban population are exposed to various levels of atmospheric pollution and the impact on human health and welfare could be explicitly incorporated into this section of the model. In an earlier study it was demonstrated that the pattern of migration at the city scale can be modelled with reasonable accuracy (Madden and Moffatt, 1980) and more recent research has revealed that 'environmental degradation of a city is directly related with the migration rate of the city' (Orishimo, 1981). It would, therefore, be possible to include environmental quality as part of the complex processes of inter-urban as well as intra-urban migration.

The economic activity section in the current model depends on inputs of energy, labour and capital. One of the major difficulties in modelling economic activity resides in the fact that exogenous influences can greatly affect the endogenous behaviour of the urban system. The decision to close down the Players cigarette factory in Stirling, for example, has both positive influences on the health of Stirling and its inhabitants but also a negative impact on the employment prospects for many townsfolk. Obviously, research into the economic structure of an urban area and related environmental pollution must devote more attention to this crucial issue (Coupe, 1976).

The land use system is the fourth sub-sector of the conceptual model. In the study of several urban areas it has been demonstrated that land use is a major determinant of environmental quality. For example, in the United States of America, Berry undertook an in-depth study of the relationships between environmental pollution and the type and intensity of urbanization in 76 centres in the United States (Berry, 1974). He demonstrated that when city-size and the level of manufacturing are held constant, then the mix and pattern of land use are the major determinants of the nature, intensity and pattern of environmental pollution. Again, in Scotland the way in which land is used in urban areas has rarely been described let alone explained and detailed empirical research is required in this area of investigation.

The interaction of economic production, energy use, consumer preferences and the pattern of land use all inter-connect to determine the level of environmental quality in an urban area. As noted in the preliminary survey, the objective conditions of the environment may not be related to the subjective condition perceived by the residents. In a study of air pollution in Sheffield, Wall notes that 'most of the Sheffield sample (people) did not regard air pollution as an important issue and it was low in their problem hierarchy' (Wall, 1974) and this is a town in which sulphur dioxide pollution is among the worst in England. It is, therefore, clear that any study of environmental quality should stress the objective conditions of the levels of pollution as well as the subjective interpretations that different groups of people may have about their conditions.

ENVIRONMENTAL PLANNING AND HUMAN WELFARE

It would, of course, be naive to suggest that different people's perception of environmental quality necessarily implies that corrective action and environmental planning would inevitably follow. Between the objective and subjective evaluations of environmental quality are political processes which, ultimately, will decide on whether or not money will be injected into maintaining or restoring the quality of the environment. Whilst Selman argues that, 'probably the major influence which planners can bring to bear in pollution is in the location of new developments such that social benefits are maximized, environmental nuisances minimized and the best uses made of the existing infrastructure' (Selman, 1977) it is not clear that politicians or entrepreneurs will listen to such advice or place it high on their list of priorities even if many people are affected adversely by such crucial locational decisions. In a study of the assessment of the urban environment in Canada and the United States, it was shown that municipal governments ranked finance as the most important priority with environmental quality and human welfare ranked as seventh and eighth respectively (Lang and Armour, 1980). Clearly, then, the decision to inject funds into maintaining or enhancing environmental quality in urban areas is essentially a political issue and this model when developed can only indicate the various social-costs and benefits associated with improving environmental quality and human welfare. This in turn leads to a brief consideration of environmental planning and human welfare in Stirling.

Over the next few years some improvements in the urban environment are planned by Stirling District Council. One of the objectives of the *Stirling Town Centre Draft Local Plan* is to 'encourage development and re-development of land and buildings currently underused so that the quality of the existing environment is maintained and enhanced' (Stirling District Council, 1978). In order to improve the quality of the environment in Stirling, several schemes have been proposed. These environmental planning proposals include an extension of the existing conservation area, predominantly the Victorian villa middle-class residential area, to cover the town centre and main shopping streets as well as to upgrade the old town and upper Bridge Street as outstanding conservation areas.

Whilst these proposals are laudable it is obvious that residents in the higher socio-economic areas of Stirling would benefit by having the quality of their good environment further enhanced whereas the people living in the objectively worst environment such as the Raploch and western Riverside will not benefit from these proposed environmental plans. It would, however, be wrong to suggest that in Stirling the socially deprived areas are to be totally ignored with regard to environmental improvement. In the Raploch area it has been estimated that the cost of making environmental improvements would be £257 400 or £2300 per house at 1981 prices which represents 2.4 per cent of the £10.5 million annual Stirling Council budget (Stirling District Council, 1981). The project is currently being funded by central government through urban aid grants up to 75 per cent of the total cost. If, however, funding were to cease, then the financial burden would rest with Stirling District Council. Whilst it is very encouraging to report on funds being available to promote a cleaner and healthier environment in Raploch, it is to be hoped that environmental planning will be a complement to, rather than a substitute for, adequate social provision (England and Bluestone, 1971). Fortunately, in the Raploch scheme the improvement of environmental quality is part of a programme to improve the quality of life.

CONCLUSIONS

This paper has reported on a preliminary study of environmental quality in Stirling. The objective and subjective surveys have revealed the spatial variations of environmental quality in the burgh and, as in other studies of larger western cities, it was demonstrated that the lower socio-economic groups experience the worst environmental quality. It must, of course, be stressed that the methods employed in this study could be further enhanced by the use of more quantitative indicators such as noise and lead pollutant levels. Unfortunately, data for enlarging this type of objective survey were not available in Stirling and further research is required using various types of environmental monitoring equipment. Similarly, the subjective study could be further enhanced by determining the ways in which various socio-economic groups and their elected representatives rank environmental issues in their list of priorities.

From this study a conceptual model has been described which illustrates the interdependencies between energy, environmental quality, economic activity, land use, demography, perception and urban politics including planning. It is suggested that this model could be developed so that various options aimed at improving environmental quality and human welfare could be evaluated. This inevitably involves considerations of the role between local urban government and the national government.

From the results of the survey it is clear that Stirling District Council have decided to channel limited financial resources to those residents in greatest need in the Raploch area. Clearly, this policy of positive discrimination follows the principle of social justice whereby increasingly scarce resources are allocated so that they bring the greatest benefit to the objectively least advantaged residents of the town (Harvey, 1973). The decision to apply this principle of social justice is, however, a political issue. Increasingly, it is becoming obvious that as servants of central government, even the well intentioned liberal policy of Stirling District Council is being threatened by the stringent cash limits imposed on the Council by the monetarist policies of the current Conservative government. The improvements in the quality of the environment in parts of Stirling have been aided by EEC funds (Haggerty, 1982). It could, of course, be argued that failure to improve the quality of the urban environment, and hence improve some aspects of human welfare, could lead to more radical political action (Hamnett, 1983). Clearly, then, there is a need for further detailed research into the changing quality of the urban environment and the impact that various policies have upon different socio-economic classes in Scottish towns and cities.

REFERENCES

Adams, J.S. (ed.) 1976. *Urban Policy making and Metropolitan dynamics. A comparative geographic analysis.* (Ballinger Press).

Berry, B.J.L. 1974. Land use, urban form and environmental quality. *Chicago Department of Geography Research Paper,* 155, (University of Chicago).

Best, R.H. 1976. The extent and growth of urban land. *The Planner,* 62(1), 8-11.

Coppock, J.T. and Wilson, C.S. 1974. *Environmental Quality,* (Scottish Academic Press).

Coupe, B.E.M.G. 1976. *Regional economic structure and environmental pollution.* Studies in Applied Regional Science, 5, Martinus Nijhoff Social Science Division.

Douglas, I. 1981. The city as an ecosystem. *Progress in Physical Geography,* 5(3). 315-361.

England, R. and Bluestone, B. 1971. Ecology and class conflict, in *Ecology Society and Man,* Allan J.D. and Harrison A.J. (eds), (Wadsworth), 31-35.

Forth River Purification Board, 1977. *Annual Report.* (Scottish Universal Newspapers).

Gordon, G. 1974. Urban Settlement, in *The Stirling Region.* Timms, D.W.G. (ed), (Stirling University), 191-220.

Haggerty, J. 1982. Putting pride back into a community. *Stirling Observer,* 31 March. 10.

Hamnett, C. 1983. The conditions in England's inner cities on the eve of the 1981 riots. *Area,* 15(1), 7-13.

Harvey, D. 1973. *Social Justice and the city.* (Arnold).

Huebner, L.A. and Paul, S.C. 1979. The Assessment of Environmental Quality. *Progress in Resource Management and Environmental Planning,* Vol. 1, O'Riordan, T. and D'Arge, R.C. (eds), (John Wiley and Sons), 179-205.

Kalma, J.D. and Newcombe, K.J. 1976. Energy use in two large cities: a comparison of Hong Kong and Sydney, Australia. *International Journal of Environmental Studies,* 9(1). 53-64.

Kapp, K.W. 1974. *Environmental policies and development planning in contemporary China and other essays.* (Mouton).

Keddie, A.W.C., Bower, J.S., Maughan, R.A., Roberts, G.H. and Williams, F.P. 1978. *The measurement, assessment and prediction of air pollution in the Forth Valley of Scotland - Final Report.* (Warren Spring Laboratory, Department of Industry).

Knox, P.L. 1976. Fieldwork in urban geography: assessing environmental quality. *Scottish Geographical Magazine,* 92(2). 101-7.

Lang, R. and Armour, A. 1980. *Environmental Planning Resource Book.* Lands Directorate, Environment Canada.

Madden, M. and Moffatt, I. 1980. The modelling of migrations in urban and regional systems, in *Simulation of Systems '79,* Dekker, L. Savastano G. and Vansteenkiste G.C., (eds), (North-Holland Publishers). 115-125.

Mandel, E. 1972. *Late Capitalism.* (Verso).

Orishimo, I. 1981. City size and environmental quality relative to population movement. *Papers of the Regional Science Association,* 46, 79-95.

O'Riordan, T. and D'Arge, R.C. (eds) 1979. *Progress in Resource Management and Environmental Planning,* 1, (John Wiley & Sons).

Pacione, M. 1980. Differential quality of life in a metropolitan village. *Transactions of the Institute of British Geographers,* New Series. 5(2), 185-206.

Perloff, H.S. (ed) 1969. *The quality of the urban environment.* (John Hopkins Press, Baltimore).

Selman, P.H. 1977. Planning for environmental quality. *Scottish Geographical Magazine,* 93(3), 168-78.

Stirling District Council, 1978. *Stirling Town Centre Draft Local Plan,* (Stirling District Council).

Stirling District Council. 1981. *Annual Budget Year 1981/82.* (Stirling District Council).

Timms, D.W.G. (ed) 1974. *The Stirling Region.* (University of Stirling).

Wall, G. 1974. Public response to air pollution in Sheffield, England. *International Journal of Environmental Studies,* 5(4), 259-70.

Wood, C.M., Lee, N., Luker, J.A. and Saunders, P.J.W. 1974. *The Geography of Pollution: A study of Greater Manchester.* (Manchester University Press).

Wood, C.M. 1979. Land use planning and pollution control, in *Progress in Resource Management and Environmental Planning,* 1, O'Riordan T. and D'Arge R.C. (eds), (John Wiley and Sons), 281-315.

Discussant's Comments

Urlan Wannop

In the papers by Moffatt, Pacione and Robertson there is a challenge
to the constituents of the urban social analyses prevalent in the
early 1970's, and to the direct translation of these analyses into administrative policy for selected parts of major urban areas in Britain.
Although Strathclyde was not the first British local authority to
undertake an areal analysis of its distribution of social deprivation,
it has kept corrective policy as a principal element in its political
strategy since 1976. In dealing with Ferguslie Park in Paisley,
Pacione and Robertson focus on a local case, bringing home the criticism raised elsewhere of the deficiencies inherent in selective area
action on urban deprivation and quality of life.

Put summarily, the debate has involved the issues of whether
selective area action can have more than a marginal effect on the real
character of deprivation, of whether it is a sufficiently effective
way of reaching a maximum of those who are deprived, of whether the
indicators by which deprivation is assessed are satisfactory and, also,
of whether localised action may sometimes insufficiently reflect current understanding of the dynamics of change within urban economies.

Ferguslie Park was itself a Community Development Project of the
1970s, one of the British programme which concluded that sustained advance in local, social and economic opportunities would arise not from
local action but from sustained improvement in the wider urban economy.
This point bears on the criticism that packages of social and physical
action within selected local areas are inefficient, so far as only a
proportion of people in any of these areas fall below the statistical
thresholds of deprivation on the chosen indicators. At the same time,
many people in need as acute as the most deprived in the most deprived
areas disappear in the areal analysis, because the statistical techniques recognise concentrations and not widely-dispersed individuals.
Pacione's investigation of what local people may most want from environmental action usefully contributes on the question of indicators.
Indicators drawn from Census tabulations have had the limitations of
being outdated, of explaining little of the circumstances of individuals, of revealing nothing of the kinds of personal preference which
Pacione considers and of providing only proxy measures on some of the
principal concerns of social policy.

On top of these difficulties, too close a focus on selected
localities must risk forgetfulness of larger forces at work in the
economic and social restructuring of urban areas. Robertson tells of
recent adjustments to policy within Ferguslie Park, leading to immediate minimal improvement of some kind in a maximum of houses by
spreading resources thinly, rather than by concentrating upon major
improvement in fewer houses. Pacione's form of survey does not go so
far as to allow it to be said that this is the policy which local
people would prefer but, from evidence from the GEAR Project in Glasgow, it is clear that sustained comprehensive environmental improvement in a run-down area can much reduce the inclination to leave of a
significant proportion of local people. There are two serious
doubts here, however. First, after progressive general improvement
in Scottish housing conditions in the past thirty years and marked
environmental improvement in the past decade, we now face the strong

possibility that Government expenditure policy will lead to setbacks
in conditions in the 1980s. Moffatt anticipates this risk in his
paper. Second, whatever the recently improved acceptability of
housing and environmental conditions in inner urban and deprived
areas of Scottish cities, there is no possibility within the 1980s
of creating jobs in these areas sufficient for local people who are
out of work. If ever the labour market does expand to include work
for those in greatest difficulty in Ferguslie Park and other deprived areas, the majority of the new jobs are likely to lie far
away in a continued restructuring of urban Britain.

Chapter 8

Aspects of Social Malaise

in Scotland

Melvyn Howe

Health, like good housing in a congenial environment, or being sufficiently educated to be able to make the most of one's abilities,
or having sufficient to eat, is one of the many indicators of quality
of life. Lack of health, or overcrowding in poor housing lacking
basic facilities, poverty, or deprivation, is one of the indicators
of social malaise. This paper will concentrate on the Scottish and
Glasgow scene with respect to these two indicators, viz. health or,
more generally, the lack of it.

Health or ill health are concepts: they are not absolute quan-
tities. In both cases standards are continually changing with the
acquisition of knowledge and the establishment of cultural objectives. Health, as defined by the World Health Organisation, is 'a
state of complete physical, mental and social well-being and not
merely the absence of disease or infirmity'. The word 'health' is
thus an evaluative term with moral, spiritual, political and social
overtones. It is not limited to bodily functioning, as is the main
concern of the medical doctor.

This WHO notion of health as man's vigorous, creative and even
joyous involvement in environment and community, of which presence
and absence of disease is only a part, has quite different implications from the mere freeing of man from disease or disorder, as
identified throughout the history of medicine. It calls for positive political action and the creation of appropriate economic and
social conditions. Indeed in many respects health may be considered
as fundamentally a political term. Such a view of health most doctors would probably be unwilling to accept, since, to adopt such an
approach to health would be to call for some movement away from in-
vesting or diverting a great part of the national resources for
remedying or curing existing illness (£11.7 billion in the UK as a
whole in 1980-81, £1.3 billion in Scotland, and £325 million in the
Greater Glasgow Health Board area) - a never ending exercise -
towards the principle of preventing, checking or controlling, through
social and political action. many of the conditions which give rise
to ill health or illness.

To be truly healthy a person should enjoy a balanced relationship
of the body and mind and complete adjustment to the total environment. It is a state of mind as well as a condition of the body;
it represents ecological balance, harmony in the environment.
Disease. on the other hand. is maladjustment in the environment. a
lack of harmony or ecological disequilibrium. All too many people
to whom one is prepared to assign the status 'ill' or 'unhealthy'
find themselves so because they are poor, grow up in bad housing,
eat poor food, work, if at all, at depressing jobs, and generally
exist on the margin of survival. In these matters the doctor is

powerless. He retains a notion of health tied to illness because
here he is all powerful. Illness is a central concept of medicine
and the doctor is the entrepreneur of illness. It is not, as already noted, a matter of objective fact but rather a term used to
describe deviation from a notional norm. A choice exists as to
whether or not to call someone ill. Is the alcoholic or the drug-
taker ill or just bad? In 1974 the American Psychiatric Association
voted and decided that homosexuality was not an illness. Yet homosexuality is as much part of social life since 1974 as it was before
that date - there has been no change in the objective facts. What
has changed is the way in which particular doctors choose to judge
it. Illness involves not merely the existence of certain facts but
also a judgement on those facts. And it is the doctor who does the
judging. Power is vested in the doctor and that power is not in-
significant. It might be suggested that society has far too long
abdicated to doctors the power to define 'health' with the result
that it is predominantly defined in terms of illness and disease.
As long as it is accepted that health is the exclusive preserve of
doctors, something only they have competence in, this state of
affairs will continue. 'There is a need for a shift in the balance
of effort from laboratory to epidemiology in recognition that improvement in health is likely to come in the future, as in the past,
from modification of the conditions which led to disease rather than
from intervention in the mechanism of disease after it has occurred'.
(McKeown, 1976). A conference of the Royal College of Physicians
held in London in 1982 demonstrated a growing recognition of this
fact by the medical profession by concluding that the primary determinant of good health is how people live rather than their medical
system. The main factors influencing how ill people are and how
they die are the result of anti-health forces, including poverty,
unemployment and lack of job satisfaction. Indeed in the view of
Ian Kennedy, BBC Reith lecturer in 1980, (Kennedy, 1981) ninety per
cent of health is a product of social, political and economic forces
which have nothing to do with medicine.

The virtual elimination of infectious diseases from Glasgow,
Scotland and elsewhere in the UK during the first half of the twentieth century was the result of remedying the environmental defects
of past ages such as polluted water supplies, lack of sanitation,
poor housing, etc. With the progressive improvement in the city
environment from the latter half of the nineteenth century came a
marked decline in deaths from typhoid, paratyphoid, diphtheria,
typhus, pneumonia, cholera, tuberculosis and other infectious diseases. This decline preceeded both the discoveries of Koch and
Pasteur in the late nineteenth century, the introduction of the germ
theory of diseases, and the introduction of therapeutic measures.
In this context recognition should be made, and credit given, to the
work of water engineers, sanitary engineers, civil engineers and
others for improvements in the environment. The traditional or
generally accepted view that doctors and medicine were, and are, the
fount from which improvements in health have flowed is, and always
was, ill-founded.

MORBIDITY

Measurement of health in official statistics and government publications are usually achieved by utilising data on rates of morbidity and mortality. Such measures are indicators of ill-health rather
than health but they provide the most feasible and readily accessible substitute.

Morbidity itself is difficult to define and the terms used to
describe it are many and varied. They include sickness, illness,

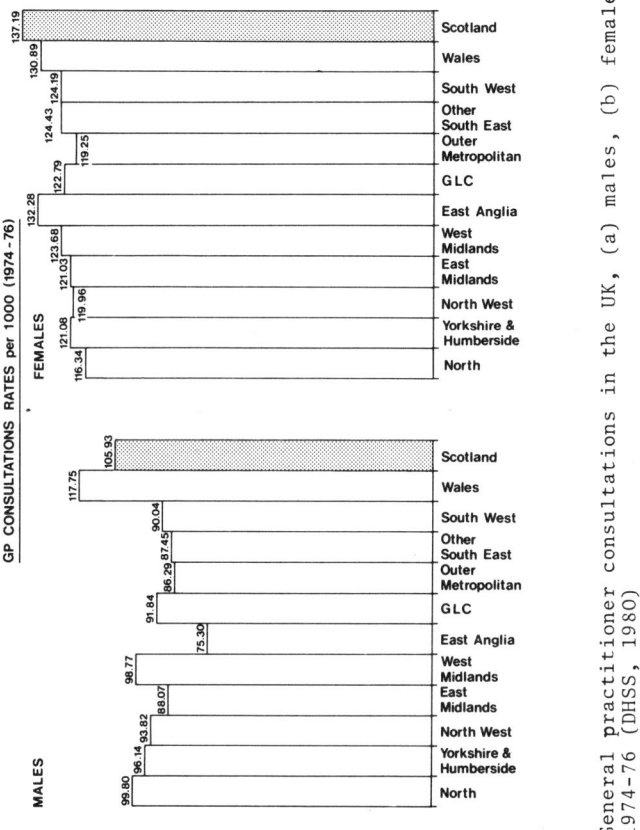

Figure 8.1 General practitioner consultations in the UK, (a) males, (b) females, 1974-76 (DHSS, 1980)

disease, injury, defect, impairment, handicap, complaint or morbid
condition. Furthermore, it is a relative state, and what may be
regarded in one country, or one place of work, or by some people, as
sufficient to justify remaining off work, or a visit to the general
practitioner or admission to hospital, may be regarded differently
in another country, or some other place of work, or among other
people. Diagnoses of morbidity in the UK are usually less detailed
or less reliable than mortality.

The General Household Survey, a multi-purpose household survey
of Great Britain with a sample size of about 30 000 persons, contains
a health section as well as a variety of socio-economic data. The
health section of the survey has each year collected data on GP
consultations, outpatient visits and illness, both of a long standing nature and also acute recent illness. What is particularly
interesting about the latter is that the data is self-reported and
self-perceived.

Figure 8.1 based on the General Household Survey (DHSS, 1980),
shows that Scotland ranks first in the UK in the numbers of GP consultations for women and second for men with, for adult males, an
increase in frequency of consultations as one goes down the scale
of social classes. Yet, interestingly, in terms of self-perceived
restricted activity, (i.e. the cutting down on activities, usually
on account of illness) Scotland, with the exception of East Anglia,
ranks lowest for both males and females relative to other parts of
the country (Figure 8.2) and has also the least long-standing illness in the UK (Figure 8.3).

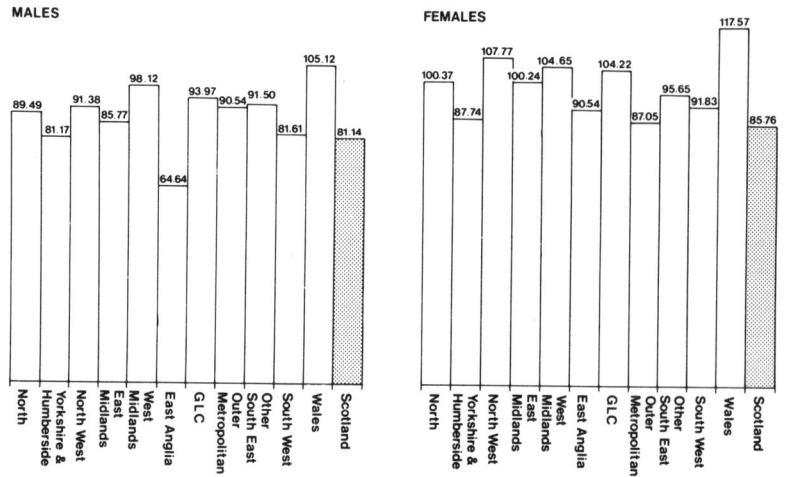

Figure 8.2   Restricted activity rates in the UK, (self-perceived
and self-reported),   (a) males, (b) females, 1974-76
(DHSS, 1980)

94

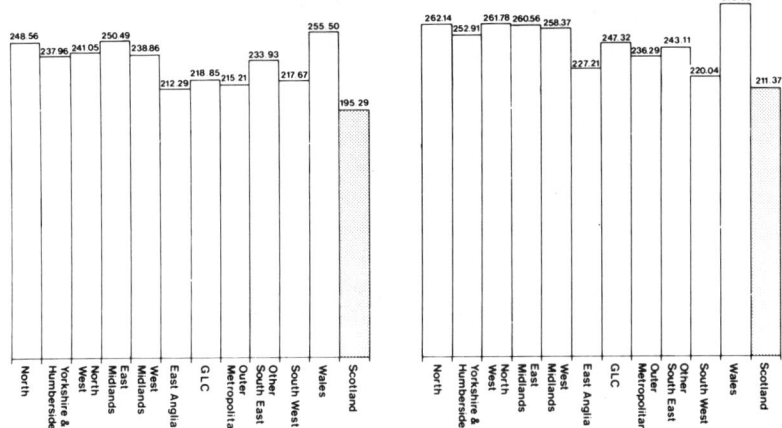

MALES   FEMALES

Figure 8.3 Long-standing illness rates in the UK (self-
            perceived and self-reported), (a) males,
            (b) females, 1974-76 (DHSS, 1980).

MORTALITY

Causes of sickness and death in the 1980s are very different from
what they were earlier in the century (Figure 8.4), and expectation
of life has greatly increased (Figure 8.5). Communicable and infectious diseases are largely a thing of the past; chronic and degener-
ative diseases have taken over. Society is now scourged by cancer,
cardiovascular disease, chronic bronchitis, mental illness and motor
vehicle accidents. In the case of each, however, there is a common
factor and this is that prevention is still very much in its infancy.
     Roughly ten per cent of early deaths occur before the age of
five years (Figure 8.4). Given that the present high level of
obstetrical and neo-natal service can be maintained it is generally
conceded that early pre-natal care, along with the early identification of high risk pregnancies, is the principal means by which
the infant mortality rate can be lowered further. The importance of
early pre-natal care is recognised more by the relatively affluent
levels of society than by the underprivileged, and this not with-
standing the fact that the availability of the National Health Service
has practically eliminated any financial barrier between a pregnant
woman and the pre-natal care she should receive. Thus it would seem
that economic circumstances, health education, attitudes, access to
health care and improved pre-natal care, are the principal factors
to be considered in lowering the rate of infant mortality.
     From five years to 35 years the principal cause of death is the
motor car accident, the second most important 'other accidents', and
the third suicide. These causes of death are mainly due to human
factors, including carelessness, impaired or dangerous driving, des-
pair and self imposed risks. Changes in these factors (e.g. the
compulsory wearing of seat belts in motor vehicles, stricter measures
to reduce the number of impaired (drunk drivers) are needed if rates
of death are to be lowered.

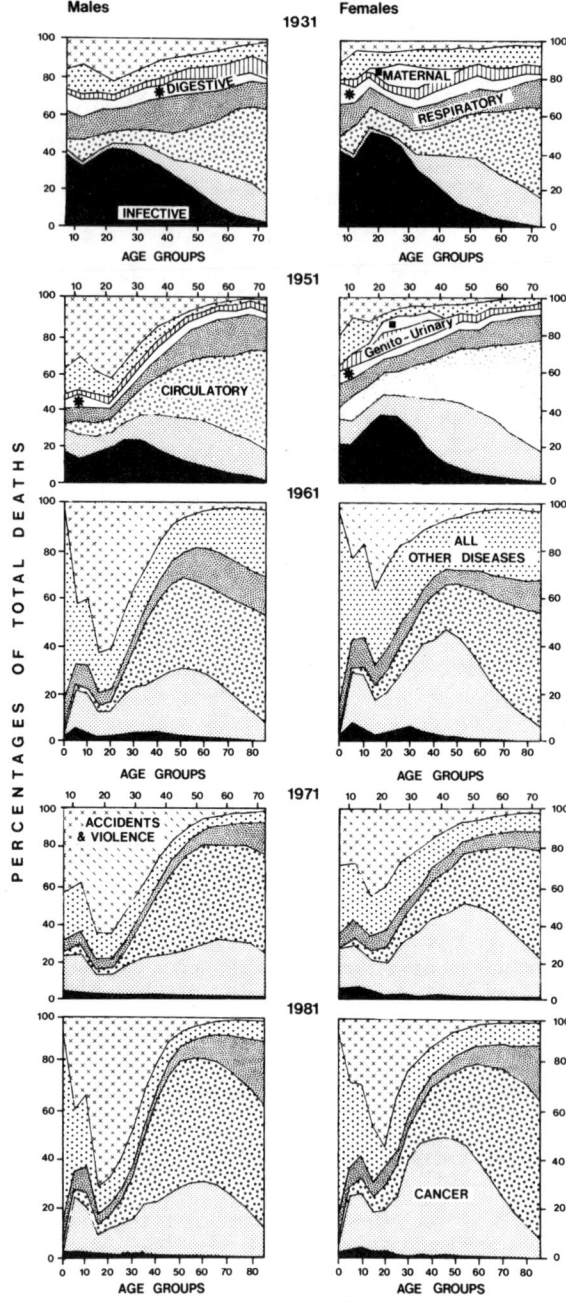

Figure 8.4   Causes of death in the United Kingdom, 1931-80 (*Social Trends*, 1982; 1983).

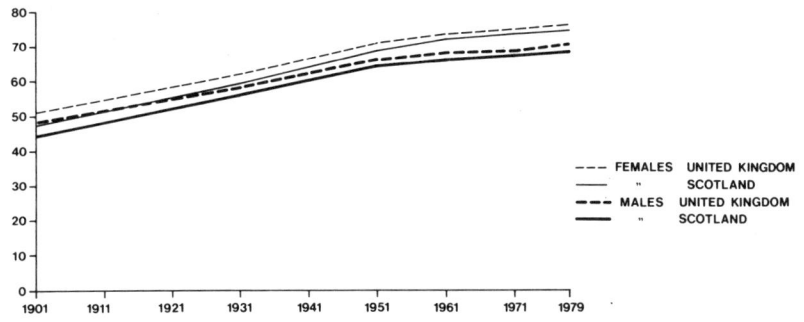

Figure 8.5   Expectation of life at birth in the United Kingdom
and in Scotland, 1901-79 (Reg. Gen. Scotland, 1982)

At 35 years diseases of the cardiovascular system (coronary
heart disease, stroke) first appear as a significant cause of death.
By the age of 40 years it becomes the principal cause and holds
that position in increasing ascendancy through all subsequent age
groups. Indeed for the age group 35-70 years diseases of the cir-
culatory system account for approximately 45 per cent of all deaths.
While the causes of these diseases are varied there seems to be
little doubt but that cigarette smoking, high fat diets, lack of
exercise, hypertension, overeating and obesity, diabetes and stress,
singly or in combination, make a dominant contribution. All of
these contributory factors are associated either with life style
(including self imposed risks) or with environmental conditions.
At 50 years the second most important cause of death is cancer
of the lung and bronchus in men and cancer of the breast, uterus
and ovaries, in women. Bronchitis, emphysema and asthma also
account for a sizeable number of deaths. With the exception of cancers of the female organs, cigarette smoking is considered to be a
major contributory factor. Once again the main cause is a self-
imposed risk.
When the full impact of lifestyle and environment on morbidity
and mortality are assessed (and the foregoing is but a partial statement of their effect) there seems little doubt but that the traditional view of equating the level of health in Scotland or Glasgow
with the availability of doctors, nurses and hospitals is inadequate.
The National Health Service, for all its facilities and for all the
numbers, training and dedication of the health professionals, still
regards the human body as a biological machine which has to be kept
in running order by removing or replacing defective parts or by
clearing its clogged lines. But for any future improvements in the
level of health of the Scots, self imposed risks have to be moder-
ated, the environment improved, and knowledge of human biology increased.
Generalised data on morbidity or mortality for Scotland or Glasgow mask the considerable class and spatial variations that exist.
Class differences (which reflect income, housing, nutrition, education and much else) are a constant feature of the entire human
lifetime. They are found at birth, during the first year of life,
in childhood, adolescence and adult life. At birth and in the first
month of life twice as many babies born to families of unskilled

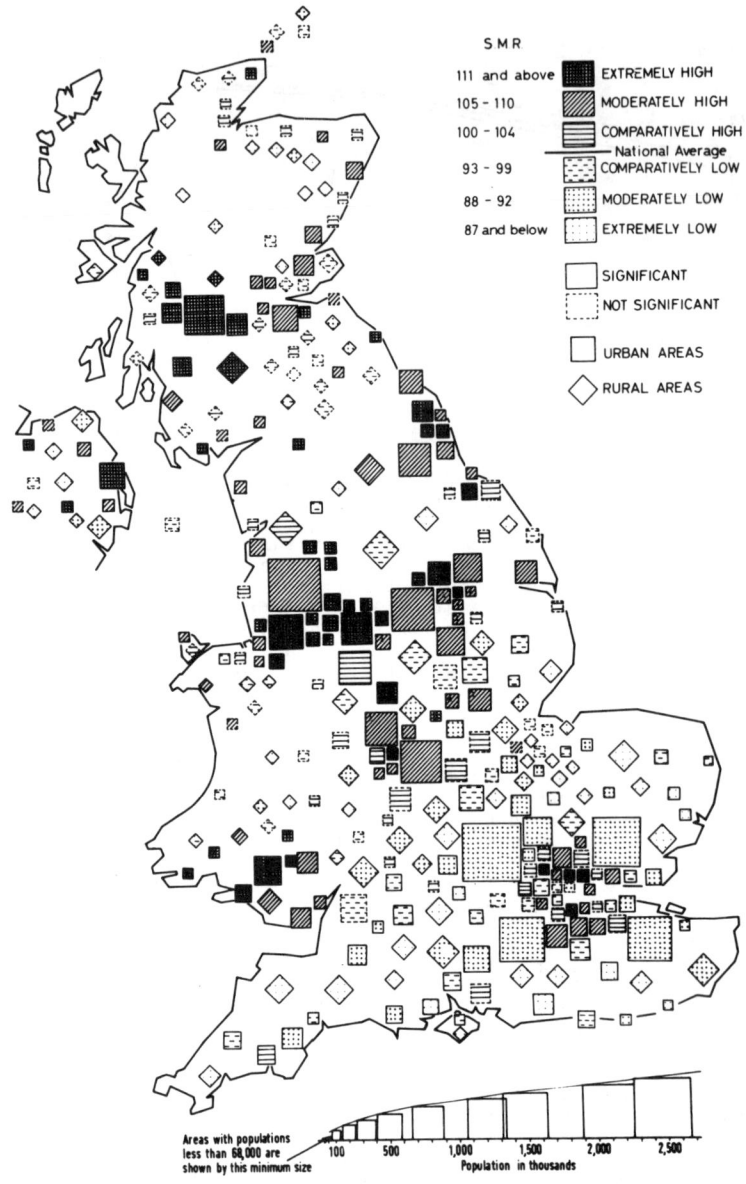

SMR

111 and above	EXTREMELY HIGH
105 - 110	MODERATELY HIGH
100 - 104	COMPARATIVELY HIGH
	National Average
93 - 99	COMPARATIVELY LOW
88 - 92	MODERATELY LOW
87 and below	EXTREMELY LOW

SIGNIFICANT

NOT SIGNIFICANT

URBAN AREAS

RURAL AREAS

Areas with populations
less than 68,000 are
shown by this minimum size

100   500   1,000   1,500   2,000   2,500
Population in thousands

Figure 8.6   Distribution of deaths from all causes in the
United Kingdom (SMR: Standardised Mortality Ratio)
(Howe, 1970)

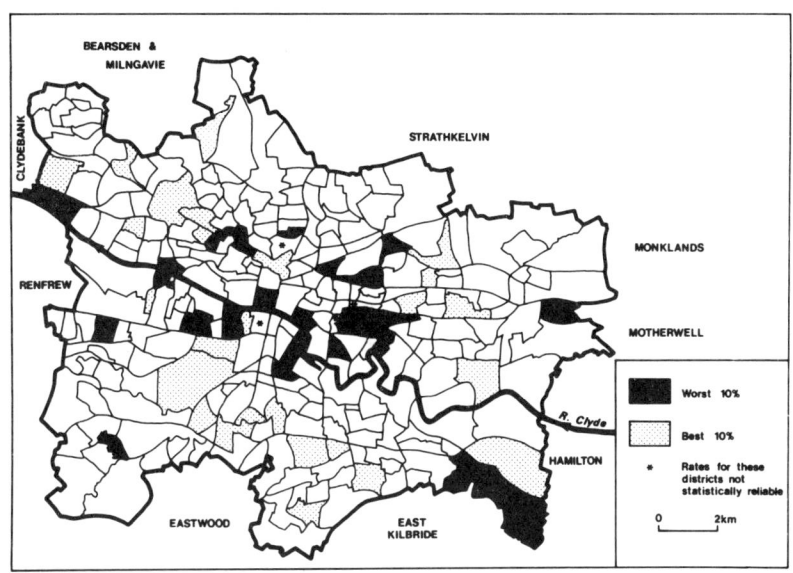

Figure 8.7a   Mortality from ischaemic (coronary) heart disease
in Glasgow, males, 35-64 years, 1975-79
(Howe and Tyndall, 1982)

manual workers die compared with those born to families in the professional class and in the next 11 months of life four times as many
girls and five times as many boys die. The cumulative impact of the
advantages and disadvantages of class differences is provided by
average life expectancy. A child born to professional parents, if
he or she is not socially mobile, can expect to spend over five
years more as a living person than a child born to an unskilled
manual household (DHSS, 1980).
    Where one lives is also important. Using mortality as an indic-
ator of health, the healthiest part of Britain is south of a line
drawn for the Wash to the Bristol Channel (Figure 8.6).
    Scotland in general has an adverse health experience compared
with most other parts of the United Kingdom and especially with the
more prosperous South of England. And within Scotland itself there
are marked inequalities; parts of Strathclyde region, and particularly Glasgow, constitute an area of unfavourable mortality experience. Yet within Glasgow mortality experience varies appreciably.
Take, for example, ischaemic (coronary) heart disease (Figure 8.7).
An analysis on the basis of 271 polling districts reveals districts
such as Kelvinside, Kelvindale, Scotstoun, Pollokshields, Newlands,
Mount Florida, Croftfoot, Burnside, Hallside, Gartcraig and North
Yoker to be relatively 'good' areas (ranked in the bottom ten per
cent) for middle-aged men (35-64 years old) for the years 1975-79,
whereas South Yoker, Ibrox, Hillhead, Anderston, Calton, Bridgeton,
Blackhill and Polmadie had the worst mortality experience for this
cause of death (ranked in the top ten per cent). There is, of course,
considerable speculation as to the role played by various factors in
bringing about coronary heart disease. The obese are prone to diabetes; people under stress take little exercise; racial and genetic
influences or regional traditions are often associated with differences in diet. Obesity, exercise and diet are themselves interrelated. When one examines the relationships or correlations between

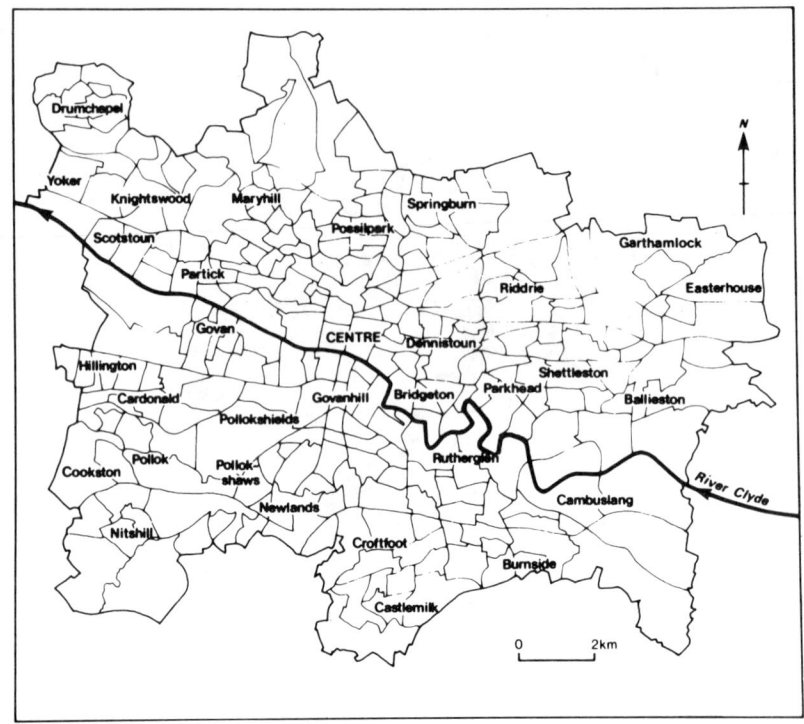

Figure 8.7b   Key to locations shown on Fig. 8.7a

coronary heart disease and individual environmental, life-style or
genetic factors it is more or less inevitable that other factors
will interfere. Causes are rarely simple or static: on the contrary
they are multi-factorial and dynamic. Evidence would suggest however that behaviour and life style are generally the spheres in
which prevention and the enhancement of health status is likely to
be achieved and that the identification of groups in the population
by social class may be expedient. When one finds that some sections
of society within Scotland or Glasgow are healthy or unhealthy relative to those living elsewhere the relationship is generally with
social class and this, in turn, relates to income, education, diet,
housing, etc. rather than to the number or availability of doctors.
Whether or not communities are healthy or unhealthy it is not due to
the presence or absence of doctors, nurses or hospitals. Figure 8.8
shows that Scotland is well-endowed in this respect.
    It would seem incumbent on the Government to seek to examine the
impact of its economic and other policies on the health and well-
being of its citizens. There is no doubt but that growing unemployment, falling living standards, stress and frustration are having a
decidedly adverse effect on the health of the people of this country.

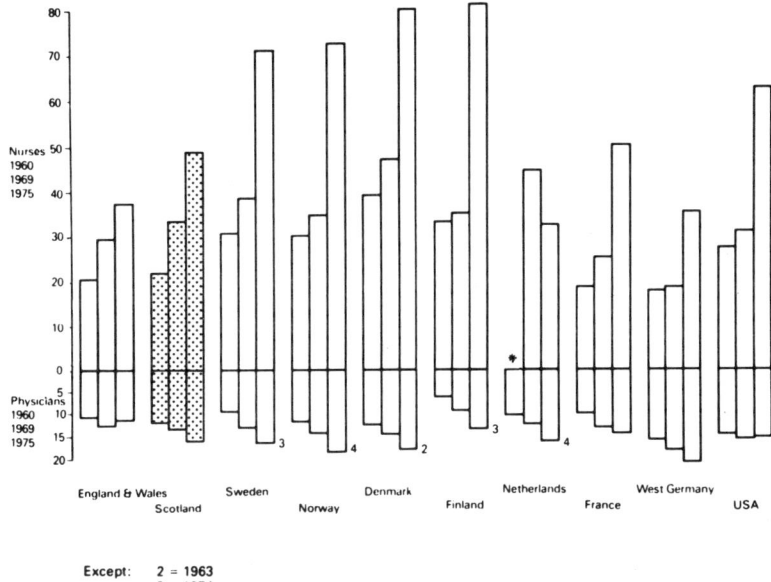

Figure 8.8   Availability of health care per 10 000 population
(Maxwell, 1974; 1981)

CONCLUSIONS

The social and spatial variations of morbidity and mortality noted
above are aspects of social malaise which deserve attention. Few
persons in authority appear to be conscious of, or anticipate environmental and occupational health hazards, and rarely, if ever,
do planners take health factors and health care into account.

It may seem expedient in the short term to give priority to
economic considerations in planning, where they relate to say industry, or to road, or rail or air communications. There is a need to
multiply wealth, to increase the gross national product in order to
acquire the income to pay for social improvements. A reduction in
mortality and morbidity rates in less favoured sectors of society,
or less favoured areas, would be of immense economic value, whether
it be in Scotland or Glasgow or elsewhere in Britain. In preventing
morbidity and premature death among the working population there are
benefits such as fewer days' absence from work, and increased amounts
of tax the people concerned will pay as a result of having a longer
and healthier working life. This pre-supposes, of course, that the
value of an individual to society depends solely on his productive
work and that his earnings are a measure of the value of his work.
Such a conclusion is ethically unacceptable. Crude economic reason-
ing, the constant bowing to the House of Mammon, overlooks a whole
range of social considerations, not least that nebulous but important
concept 'quality of life' which in turn depends on such consider-

ations as health, population pressure, social security, fulfilment of individual needs, job satisfaction and several other social indicators.

Planners and medical men, in their several ways though preferably in a concerted and co-ordinated effort, should examine critically areas of ill-health and social deprivation, the areas where death rates are relatively high and life expectancy relatively low. They should advise on measures thought most likely to bring about an amelioration in such areas and supervise their implementation, whether the measures are remedial or preventive.

Human progress needs to be judged by social as well as economic criteria. The provision of an improved environment is a prerequisite for a healthier nation. Society should not be satisfied until the prospects of existence, of life expectancy and quality of life for individuals are comparable in every part of the country and in every walk of life. Surely 'a state of complete physical, mental and social well-being' is everyone's birthright.

REFERENCES

Central Statistical Office, 1982. *Social Trends,* 13, (HMSO).

Central Statistical Office, 1983. *Social Trends,* 14, (HMSO).

Department of Health and Social Services, 1980. *Inequalities in Health.* Report of a Research Working Group (under the chairmanship of Sir Douglas Black).

Howe, G.M. 1970. *National Atlas of Disease Mortality in the United Kingdom,* (Thomas Nelson, London).

Howe, G.M. and Tyndall, R. 1982. 'Coronaries' in Glasgow. *Gazette,* (University of Strathclyde, 2nd Term, Glasgow).

Information Services Division, Common Services Agency for the Scottish Health Service. 1982. *Scottish Health Statistics, 1980,* (HMSO).

Kennedy, I. 1981. *Unmasking of Medicine.* (Allen and Unwin, London).

McKeown, T. 1976. *The modern rise of population.* (Edward Arnold, London).

Maxwell, R. 1974. *Health Care - The Growing Dilemma: needs versus resources in Western Europe, the United States and the USSR.* (McKinsey, New York).

Maxwell, R. 1981. *Health and Wealth: An International Study of Health Care.* (Lexington).

Office of Population Censuses and Surveys, Social Survey Division, 1982. *General Household Survey 1980,* Series GHS. No.10, (HMSO).

Registrar General Scotland, 1982. *Annual Reports, to Annual Report 1981,* No. 127, (HMSO).

Chapter 9

Health in Glasgow:

The Influence of Behaviour and Environment

Gordon Stewart

One of the new axioms which has emerged in the post-boom era of the
affluent and consumer societies is that health is not a commodity
which can be created by technology or purchased by affluence.
Neither is it a birthright which can be taken for granted in human
societies. It is increasingly seen to be a product of environment
and behaviour, personal and communal, within that environment,
wherever it may be. Because of this, geographers have become part
of the health profession because of their knowledge of place as a
factor influencing states of health. The Department of Geography
in the University of Strathclyde has been foremost in the United
Kingdom and prominent internationally in promoting this concept and
in developing their subject accordingly.

In its application to health, place is larger than its mere
acreage or regional definition. It includes much of what is going
on in that place, longitudinally through the history and development of human society in that place. Glasgow is the kind of place
which is especially appropriate to study the subject because so much
of its social and cultural development, good and bad, is a matter
of record and because it offers so many lessons in the opportunities
and pitfalls of social evolution. In the beginning, there was of
course a simple prehistoric community about which we know little
except that it got a place in the world map by a few early and tre-
mendously important happenings - early settlement as a riverside
community; fortification by the Romans under Antoninus (AD 148);
foundation of a cathedral and status as a city (AD 1100); foundation
of one of its two universities (AD 1451); establishment of mediaeval
trades and guilds, including a medical profession which became col-
legiate in 1655. It was already a centre of substance and character
in its pre-industrial status. This gave an extra strength and quality to its industrial development which, as in religion, urban organisation and academic resource, was ahead of the field in the post-
renaissance European league. The character, potential and fate of
the city were to a large extent predetermined in those days, as was
the subsequent environment and behaviour of its citizens.

If we look at Glasgow today, it presents an almost absurd mixture of development and collapse, of vitality based on decay, which
is incomprehensible unless we fill in the historical as well as the
geographic dimension. In matters of health, we stand unequivocally
and unenviably very low indeed in the European league, starting with
bad figures for infancy and child health, proceeding through a
greater frequency of avoidable diseases in middle age to a shorter
expectation of life than anywhere else in the developed world. We
are in fact showing the rest of the world how easy it is to go back-
wards in terms of health and welfare because we are retaining and

even encouraging diseases and threats to health which have disappeared or are diminishing elsewhere. We have a high frequency of
other common but, nevertheless, avoidable diseases like caries,
chronic bronchitis, coronary heart disease, alimentary and lung
cancer; most of our industries show high illness-absence rates and,
as a society, we have a quite fantastic preoccupation with sickness
and medicines. These problems are common everywhere as residues of
earlier hazards and ways of life but the badge of progress elsewhere
is the civic, communal and personal enlightenment that comes with
awareness of causes and, consequently, of corrective behaviour. In
Glasgow, this is lacking. The difference between Amsterdam or Copen-
hagen or other northern cities and Glasgow, equivalent in size,
antiquity, latitude and development, is that in Amsterdam and Copen-
hagen, as in Holland and Scandinavia generally, they have learned
the elementary grammar of health education whereas in Glasgow, by
and large, we have not. We could say, a few years ago, that in
these other cities they were worried about the use of narcotic drugs
but now we have this worry too.

In my presentation to the symposium, I tried to spell out some
of this in demographic and epidemiological terms. Part of the story
is well told, and to some extent summarised, by indicator statistics,
such as the infant mortality rate. In Glasgow, the overall figure
is about 15 infant deaths per 1000 live births, which is respectable
though higher than the UK average but the overall figure conceals
the range which is 8-12 in the better districts and 30 or more in
the worst. Hospital figures (Table 9.1) show that about 70 per cent
of infants admitted come from the 40 per cent who live in the new
housing estates such as Castlemilk, Drumchapel, Easterhouse and
Garthamlock. That is to say, from architecturally-original, compre-
hensively planned estates built since 1955 in a bold and costly
attempt to correct the bad housing which, before that, was thought
to be the cause of the problem. Yet the familiar infectious diseases
of childhood, such as measles, gastro-enteritis, chickenpox and
whooping cough (Table 9.2) are still more prevalent in these areas
in which they readily spread in nurseries and schools and from which
they are carried by older children to other parts of the city.
Dysentery and tuberculosis are two diseases which have been wholly
eliminated in many parts of Britain but which persist in Glasgow and
Strathclyde. Tuberculosis nowadays can be prevented, or detected
early and can be cured but in the backward pockets in Glasgow it has
never been eradicated from the adult population especially in elderly
males. We are seeing also a recurrence of infestations like scabies
in children and pubic or head lice in adults which were on the point
of disappearance about thirty years ago and have wholly disappeared
from many areas since 1960.

Advances in medicine, especially in the development of vaccines,
of new anti-microbial drugs and life-support techniques, have produced a situation where most infectious diseases can be cured fairly
rapidly. This advantage does not extend sufficiently to prevention
and obscures the fact that the occurrence and severity of infection
are determined by prior events and conditions which relate, not to
medical services but to living conditions and behaviour. In Glasgow,
medical services are highly developed: there are in fact more general
practitioners, with smaller lists, many more specialists and more
hospital beds per capita of population than in any other major city
in Britain outside central London, where private medicine for other
reasons is a competitive growth industry. But, for the reasons
stated, this excess of doctors and hospital facilities makes little
if any difference because these medical services are almost wholly
preoccupied with treatment whereas the problem lies in detection and
prevention, much less by medical means than by education of children
and their parents in avoidance of disease and maintenance of health.
To prevent infectious diseases, the education has to be at an elemen-

Table 9.1   Areas of deprivation in Glasgow 1981

Deprivation variables (percentages of:)	Postcode District			
	G15	G14	G51	G52
Children (0 - 14 years incl.)	29	19	17	24
Households with dependent children	33	36	19	34
" " 4 or more children	9	4	7	5
" " permanently sick persons	3	3	3	2.5
" overcrowded	19	20	20	8
" lacking basic amenities	3	12	9	6
% of hospital admissions for respiratory infections	12	2.4	3.4	0.9
Unemployment	15%	15%	25%	12.8%

Note: about 18% admissions from 3 out of 43 postcode districts in survey area, i.e. from only 11% of population of children at risk.

Table 9.2   Hospital admissions for whooping cough* in Glasgow 1976-82. Demographic and social variables

Districts surveyed	No. of children In district (%)	(<15 years) No. admitted (%)	Admissions per 1000
Deprived	73,798 (43%)	382 (66%)	5.2
Non-deprived	97,054 (57%)	198 (34%)	2.0
All districts surveyed	170,852	580	3.4

*Whooping cough syndrome.   B. pertussis isolation rate 35%

Note that 66% of admissions come from the 43% of the population in deprived districts.

---

tary level: toilet-training, hand washing, hygiene in bathroom and kitchens, personal towels, clean clothing, disinfection of contaminant materials and premises, and so forth. This requires observance and action on a personal level at home and at a communal level in schools and public places.

Disinfection is assisted by ventilation, abundant water and sunlight, retarded by closed windows, dampness, indoor and artificial life styles. Children learn bad habits as readily as good ones, and what they learn in childhood tends to stay with them as a life style, especially if they remain in the same community. In Glasgow, the life style of the former slums have been transferred to the new housing estates, hence the same problems persist.

Infectious diseases and disorders of infancy and childhood are important as indicators because they point to places and vulnerable groups where efforts on the educational, environmental, social and medical fronts require intensification. But these diseases are only part of the problem, the greater part of which is the burden of chronic disease and low level of fitness in the adult population. Much of this is attributable to disorders which are disabling rather than lethal and which have a strong, if not always obvious, psychological component in so far as they are incurable without a conscious will to betterment on the part of the sufferer. Chronic bronchitis, obesity, arthritis, various ailments of digestion, alcoholism, drug-abuse and various kinds of depression all come into this category. These are the illnesses which lead people to their general practitioners, usually to receive drugs which may relieve the symptoms but not the cause and which create simultaneously a dependence and a burden upon the health services. The influence of personality and life-style in the maintenance of such diseases is now well-recognised, largely because of the self-evident effects of cigarette-smoking upon cardiovascular and respiratory fitness, but the lesson has not been equally well learned even by educated sections of the public or, perhaps for that reason, by decision makers in the health services. The delusion persists that health is something which has to be provided, organised and purchased, and is therefore costly and technical. The essential truth that it is largely a personal responsibility from childhood onward is hard to tell and almost impossible to sell, especially in a population which views itself as deprived, dependent and incapable of helping itself. Harsh as these words may seem, they describe the mentality of many people in the new slums of many cities and especially of Glasgow. This state of mind is transmissible, as readily or more readily than any infectious disease. When transmitted through a generation, it becomes chronic and endemic, more persistent than tuberculosis, much more difficult to cure, impossible to eradicate without a process of psychological disinfection at all levels in that community, not least in those who foster dependence upon ineffective remedies and retreats.

For a time, it looked as though full employment and prosperity would bring their own solutions to some of these problems by closing the poverty trap and liberating poorer people to seek a fuller life style. In many parts of Europe, especially in the industrial ghettoes of northern Italy, France and Belgium, and in the ravaged cities of Germany, this proved to be true. But not in Glasgow which preserved its slums and slum mentality through the years of industrial expansion and prosperity, right through the sixties in to the early seventies, by which time the new housing estates had become new slums with a bewildering array of new problems to add to the substantial residue inherited from former years. Anyone who knows Glasgow knows also that the problem areas are constructed almost entirely of relatively new houses in situations which are geographically attractive. The essence of the local problem is the unique ability in these areas to recreate the hazards of the past in the salubrious environment of the present. There is much more which needs to be said and done about the health states of the city and conurbation but it can all be summed up in the differences in health statistics between, say, Milngavie, Bearsden, Whitecraigs and Newton Mearns on the one hand and Easterhouse, Castlemilk, Drumchapel and Blackhill

on the other. These statistics, unlike some others, do not lie.
They are the hard end-points of a habit which in these areas has
become a tradition: a habit of neglect of attention to personal,
family and communal hygiene, of low drive toward improvement of self
or locality, of resistance to any change and of apathy about the
dilemma of youth and the dismal prospects for those of all ages.
The immediate outcome is visible in the form of inane graffiti in
dirty entrances, uncultivated gardens used as middens, continuous
vandalism, broken doors and windows, abandoned homes. Shops, transport and other services and amenities have to be withdrawn. Schools
and recreation deteriorate, maintenance fails to keep pace with
rising costs and the area becomes 'deprived'. Meanwhile, the birth
rate stays high, the unemployed stay put, those who want to move
can't because they won't get a council house elsewhere, so the problems intensify. In Liverpool, Toxteth and elsewhere, ethnic differences contribute to the stress but this dimension is fortunately
lacking in Glasgow where the immigrants have no difficulty in out-
witting the locals in starting new enterprises ingeniously geared to
the low standards and general backwardness of the local scenario.
    It would be grievously wrong to paint this picture without ack-
nowledging the fierce respectability and tenacity of some of the inhabitants of these 'deprived' districts, or without mentioning the
efforts by groups of tenants in several parts of the east end and
in Maryhill to promote self-help and provide cultural stimulation.
It is characteristic in Glasgow - it is indeed a paradoxical part
of the same tradition - to find bright shafts of optimism and ori-
ginality in the greyness. We drew attention to this in our 'Under-
view' report of 1978 but we felt then, and I feel still, that the
impact of such efforts is also paradoxical, being maximal in intel-
lectuals in the west end and minimal in the deprived localities.
There are very few examples in Scottish history of an effective
counter-culture to conformism since the days of the Covenanters,
but plenty of examples of exploitation of these who too readily con-
form to conditions which, in a literate society elsewhere, would be
unacceptable. It is foolish to attempt to quantify social parameters beyond a certain point but it could be argued that, numer-
ically, addiction to alcohol, to tobacco, to spectator status and
now to drugs, swamps local efforts and impedes central efforts to
correct cultural decay.
    As a study in social geography, these sharp differences in the
appearance and underlying reality of quality of living in various
parts of Glasgow are fascinating. But the gap between the worst and
the rest is not lessening and, in some respects, widening especially
in the increase in crime and drug abuse, in neglect of children and
of the need to create or recreate opportunities for youth in gainful
and rewarding activity, to say nothing of employment. To recognise
this gap and do nothing, or the little that amounts to nothing,
about it is no longer simply an acceptance of deprivation or laissez-
faire pragmatism. It is a positive complacency as bad or worse than
the apathy beneath. Correction politically is not the remit of this
paper but health affairs are, and rightly so, because repair of some
of the main defects in this field is possible. It is a matter of
learning how, in educational, economic and political terms, in that
order, to bridge the sad and persisting gap. This means dealing
with difficulties which are inbred not only in people but also in
the structure and orientation of our system of health maintenance
and delivery of health care.
    The reorganisation of municipal and county councils and of health
boards in Britain in 1974-75 was intended to overcome some of these
difficulties by creating new authorities which would be more efficient in management and delivery of the health and welfare services,
of housing, education and regional planning. Certainly there were
anomalies and overlaps which required correction but it is now

apparent that our new and vastly expanded bureaucracies are no more
able than their predecessors to deal with the extra stresses created
by unemployment upon the underlying environmental defects and social
malaise of the industrial towns of Britain. In Strathclyde, it
could be argued that reorganisation has intensified the problems of
management because responsibility for housing, social work, education, and health are now divided between three or more authorities.
The schism is particularly serious in health affairs because the six
new health boards have no direct responsibility for environmental or
occupational health, which are split between the Region, the central
Department of the Environment and the Employment Medical Advisory
Service. Public health has been virtually abandoned as a medical
responsibility, with a consequent loss of expertise and executive
activity in matters of disease control. Despite the numerous reforms
and reorganisations promoted in the National Health Service Acts of
1948, 1972 and subsequently, there has been no enactment providing
funds and authority for eliminating health hazards in housing since
1897. The only way in which an unhealthy premises can be legally
evacuated or declared to be a health hazard is by declaring, and
getting the various authorities concerned to agree to declare and to
recognise, a 'nuisance' in the language of the 1897 Act. The machinery of repair is therefore obsolescent and creaking, but it is nevertheless functional and all we have until we summon sufficient interest and social conscience to re-write the NHS Acts in terms of
health instead of sickness and dependence.
    Glasgow is by no means the only city in Britain to show, in
health statistics and in more obvious ways, the calamitous impact
of the deprivation-dependence duality upon tens of thousands of its
citizens. Liverpool, the industrial part of the north ⌐ast, South
Wales and other areas all show the same sorry picture of a continuing
and anachronistic division between two broad groups of population.
It is no longer a question simply of rich and poor because many of
the deprived were comparatively rich, on shift work in mechanised
industries, until they became unemployed. Nor is it entirely a
question of amenities because in the new housing estates like Easterhouse in Glasgow or Huyton in Liverpool, amenities are available,
in homes and schools, which would have been luxuries in affluent
households thirty years ago. It is a matter primarily of behaviour
and attitudes and of how these affect group dynamics so as to create
or maintain a subculture of socially-defiant, self-defeating activity.
This is the psychological spanner in the otherwise functional machinery and this is how Glasgow, forgetting its history, stays where it
is. In this respect, the defect lies less in the deprived areas
than in the unnatural and absurd division of society into sub-sets
with conflicting interests. This, in the second half of the twentieth century, is a peculiarly British relic, hopelessly outdated
but, like pageantry, with a following among those who live in the
past. The remedy requires re-education out of this way of thinking
and behaving. It is very unfortunate that in Glasgow, where the
democratisation of all forms of learning began so early, the process
of re-education is delayed until so late. In health affairs, this
is especially unfortunate for Glasgow was one of the first cities to
acknowledge the priorities of public health in civic policy and in
medical organisation.
    The scope of the symposium is wider than the problems of an in-
dividual city or even region. But what has been said here about
Glasgow applies in many respects to any of the older, large industrial cities in Britain and to many of the peri-urban areas where
the intention of the authorities and the planners employed by them
was to create geographic entities which would have the amenities of
cities without their problems. Yet it is precisely in those areas
that the problems of the inner cities are being reduplicated with
the additional problem of remoteness from the central districts

where, despite the hardships, a sense of identity and common interest prevailed. The failure to preserve this is a root cause of the alienation and therefore of the insensate vandalism and self-abuse which are the symbols of protest about and, simultaneously, of failure to provide better societies in new estates and communities. Unemployment and lack of opportunity or will to find opportunity at all levels are undoubtedly adding new dimensions of divisiveness and widening the rift between those who are trapped in the deprivation-dependence duality and those who are, or think they are independent and self-propelling.

This brings me to my concluding point which is that the dependence is no longer one-sided. When the economy slumps or when resources are insufficient, those who are already deprived or unskilled or lacking prospects become more so. The state uses them as such as the buffer to absorb tidal oscillations in the economy and, having used them, continues to do so because they are least able to resist or escape. The dilemma of the deprived and dependent populations in British cities can then be seen as a small scale representation of the huge human dilemma of a third world amid two others, of south and north, of an inhuman gulf which human institutions, resources and technology might bridge but chooses instead to leave, as a non-geographic cleavage of planet Earth. The social relativity scale ensures that this gulf will remain because deprivation in British or European or North American cities, bad as it is, cannot compare with that in Ethiopa or Bangladesh or about two-thirds of the world where the per capita income of the employed is vastly lower than that of the unemployed in the other third. This is so because, as long as these gross differences exist in the developed world where knowledge and resources for correction are available, they will remain and intensify elsewhere on such a scale as, perhaps, to confound any possibility of correction. There is more than a local reason for looking critically at the problems of a city like Glasgow.

Chapter 10

The Detection of Mutagenic Compounds

in the Aqueous Environment

David Milne

INTRODUCTION

The effects on society of mutagens in the environment are primarily
two-fold. The first is the direct effect where mutagenic compounds
- which are mainly a by-product of contemporary technology - are
absorbed and/or adsorbed by man. The majority of carcinogens are
mutagens (Ames, 1973) (estimated at over 90 per cent) and therefore
environmental exposure to mutagens presents a risk of the possible
induction of cancer. The International Association for Research on
Cancer currently estimates that over 80 per cent of cancers have
some environmental link and according to Lewin (1976) it is now pro-
bable that mutagenic compounds in the environment cause about 90 per
cent of all cancers. As a result of these statements the development of mutagen screening must surely accelerate in the 1980s. The
value of mutagen screening concerning the aforementioned direct
effect is in two major areas. In the first instance, as a prevent-
ative measure in screening compounds before they are integrated into
industrial processes etc. and hence almost certainly into the environment. Secondly, to screen the environment and expose any compounds now present that could be shown to have mutagenic properties.
The second effect of mutagens on society is the indirect, this involves the mutagenesis of pathogenic organisms in the environment.
Such alterations in the genetic make-up can be extremely harmful to
man. One of the most important aspects resulting from mutagenesis
is the increase in antibiotic resistance. Multiple antibiotic resistance is already present in some pathogenic strains before they
are exposed to environmental mutagens. This could set the scene for
the appearance of super-multiple strains.
In addition to the direct and indirect effects, the existence
of super-mutagens gives rise to further concern. They are chemicals
that initiate high frequencies of mutations without displaying signs
of visible damage to the cell or organism. Consequently, there is
a possibility that such chemicals might well escape the more traditional toxicological screening procedures or would never be tested
at all. These induced alterations in the reproductive cells may be
passed on into future generations and are not expressed as long as
the same gene on the other chromosome is normal. Mutagens could pos-
sibly increase the number of latent abnormalities in the gene pool
of a population and result in an increase in the rate of expression
of genetic defects in future generations. Such a degeneration of
the gene pool must be avoided where practicable since it is a permanent and irreversible process.

Exploratory experiments in the late sixties exhibited the ubiquitous presence of mutagenic compounds as they were identified among food preservatives, pesticides, drugs, cosmetics and industrial chemicals. These findings, that there are many mutagenic compounds with extensive human exposure, resulted in an explosive development in the field of chemical mutagenesis which, during the last decade, has attained a new dimension as 'environmental mutagenesis' or 'genetic toxicology'. Although this expansion has taken place there have been no large scale, routine, screening programmes initiated.

MUTAGEN/CARCINOGEN DETECTION SYSTEMS

The methods of mutagen/carcinogen detection can be classified into three main groups:

i)   Epidemiological studies (carcinogen)

ii) Animal studies (carcinogen)

iii) Bacterial studies (mutagen)

Epidemiological studies are based on the incidence of various types of cancer in genetically similar human populations in different environments. This is most satisfactorily performed when immigrant groups are compared with those in their country of origin e.g. Japanese women in the USA have a higher incidence of breast cancer than those in Japan. The environmental link in cancer incidence appears to be linked to differing levels of exposure to cancer-promoting agents in different environments. There is much evidence, at present, that exposure to some chemicals can produce cancers. Although epidemiological studies are the most direct way of exhibiting a correlation between exposure to particular compounds and the occurrence of cancer in humans, they are subject to numerous limitations. a) They can only be conducted after the suspect compounds have been widely disseminated. b) They are carried out over a long time scale, as there is often a considerable delay between exposure to a carcinogen and development of a tumour. c) They are very expensive. d) There are often difficulties in identifying and matching populations. e) The demonstration of a correlation between two factors is not necessarily proof of cause and effect.

Animal studies have been the traditional alternative procedure for carcinogen detection. This involves the inoculation of materials into suitable test animals and the demonstration of induced tumours, following exposure. This system allows substances to be tested before they are widely disseminated in the environment and as test animals usually have much shorter life spans these tests do not take as long to complete as epidemiological studies. However, the approach is expensive, time consuming and requires a large number of animals; also the need to extrapolate the results of animal studies to man requires great care. The difficulties inherent in maintaining animal house facilities and the tight Home Office control on establishments performing tests on live animals has meant that work in this field has been largely restricted to universities and large commercial concerns. This means that the standard conventional laboratory would be unable to investigate carcinogens in the environment by employing animal studies.

Currently, assay systems using bacteria as test organisms are widely used as mutagen detectors. Although bacteria are far removed from man on the evolutionary scale, the inherited material is composed of DNA in both cases. These tests can be performed very quickly and cheaply in comparison with long term animal tests and the conventional microbiology laboratory can be set up to perform the assays with minimal cost and reorganisation. It involves monitoring the extent of DNA damage using the induction of mutants rather than cancer as an end point. The emphasis of this paper falls on the use and potential future use of these bacterial assay tests.

The two species of bacteria commonly used are *Salmonella typhimurium* and *Escherichia coli*. The strains are based on a 'reverse mutation system' e.g. an initial strain was able to synthesise histidine (an amino acid) but various mutant strains were isolated which had lost this ability and became histidine-dependent i.e. requiring this amino acid to be supplied in the growth medium before they could grow. These mutant strains spontaneously revert to histidine-independence. The cells are challenged with the test agent and if there is a significant increase in the rate at which bacteria regain the ability to synthesise histidine, the test agent may be mutagenic. This is only one example and other species and strains employ different amino acids in the system. Most short term tests are based on reverse, rather than forward mutations as these are frequently easier to detect and quantify. Five of the most commonly used strains of *Salmonella typhimurium* can detect different types of mutational events. This is of immense importance as certain mutagens induce specific mutational events and therefore by using all five strains in a test the complete spectrum of mutagen induction is examined. These strains have also been modified to increase the sensitivity of the assay. The cell wall structure is different from normal bacteria and test chemicals are able to penetrate the cell more easily. In addition, one of the DNA repair systems has been deleted; if this was not so the majority of the damage inflicted by the agent could be repaired by the cell and fewer mutations would be detected.

The development of these bacterial assay tests does not obviate the need for epidemiological investigations and animal exposure testing, but they have provided a powerful tool for the tentative identification of 'potential' carcinogens and to enable the conventional laboratory to investigate the occurrence of possible carcinogens in the environment.

INVESTIGATIONS OF MUTAGENS/CARCINOGENS IN THE AQUEOUS ENVIRONMENT

The Environmental Protection Agency in the USA has identified 1258 chemicals(Shackleton and Keith, 1976) present in 33 different types of water. In 1977 a report (Simmons *et al.*, 1977) on the mutagenic action of 71 of the 300 chemicals so far identified in drinking water, showed that 34 per cent had a mutagenic effect in bacterial assay tests. However, this may not represent a true proportion as low molecular weight compounds, mainly halogenated, were selected and a large proportion of these would be expected to be active.

Several epidemiological studies have been carried out in the USA in an attempt to establish if drinking water source affects the incidence of cancer in the population. The two most renowned projects are in Ohio (Kuzma and Buchner, 1977) and Louisiana (Page, Harris and Epstein, 1976). Some parishes in Louisiana draw their drinking water almost entirely from the Mississippi in which compounds known to be mutagenic have been identified. The incidence of cancer in these parishes, was compared with adjacent ones which received their drinking water from alternative sources. The result was that after many variables had been taken into account, the authors calculated that there was significantly more chance of some groups contracting cancer of the urinary organs and gastro-intestinal tract when drinking water was derived from the Mississippi River. It must be stated that some other scientists (Ames, Lee and Durston, 1973) have not placed so much significance on these data.

113

In a similar manner cancer rates in 88 counties in Ohio were correlated with the origin of their drinking water supplies - either predominately ground (42 counties) or surface (46 counties) derived. The incidence of cancer was found to be higher in the counties served by surface-derived sources. Small-scale epidemiological surveys such as these, whilst not proving an effect, suggest that it is worth investigating the biological action of organic chemicals present in water sources.

The Severn-Trent Water Authority (Tye and Waite, 1980), by employing sophisticated, chemical analytical techniques, have identified about 200 organic chemicals in water samples. Bacterial mutagenicity tests are presently being performed on these compounds using highly pure commercially-purchased samples and positive results have been obtained e.g. Dichloromethane. A series of concentrations of the test compounds have been used and this renders the assay test more certain because the resulting dose-response curve confirms that the increase in mutation rate brought about by the test substance is proportional to its concentration. Although the bacterial tests on pure compounds provide an indication of the possible biological effects of chemicals, they deal with high concentrations of chemicals in isolation. The combinations of compounds which occur in the environment and the interactions between them can either enhance or diminish their separate effects.

A preliminary, mutagenic screening study has recently been carried out on the Firth of Clyde (MacLean, 1979) employing the common mussel as the test medium instead of Clyde water. The reason for this is basically two-fold. a) As mature organisms they have a sessile mode of life which makes them a good indicator at a specific site. b) As they are filter-feeders and have an intracellular (phagocytic) mode of digestion they tend to accumulate pollutants in their tissues to higher levels than sea water. Six sites were chosen:

i) Loch Fyne (off Inveraray) - the control (clean) site.

ii) Woodhall   )all
    Newark Castle   )visually
    Prince's Pier (Greenock)   )polluted

iii) Rhu   )visually
     Ardeer (Ayrshire)   )unpolluted

The control site gave negative results. Newark Castle and Prince's Pier - both visually polluted - gave positive results. The two visually unpolluted sites, Ardeer and Rhu, also exhibited positive results and this implies that a visually clean site need not be free of mutagenic contaminants. The remaining site, Woodhall, gave a negative result which indicates that visual pollution does not guarantee mutagenic activity. It must be emphasised that this was only a preliminary study and other tests should be carried out to give more conclusive results, i.e., when a positive result is obtained, a dose-response curve should be constructed to illustrate at what concentration mutagenicity is induced. In addition, a death curve should be drawn up to see how many cells are killed at each dose rating; also chemical analyses would be necessary to characterise the mutagenic agent(s) present in the sample. This preliminary study should be the catalyst for more extensive work to be carried out on the Firth of Clyde and, as a result, a research programme has been drawn up jointly by the Clyde River Purification Board and Paisley College of Technology but as yet no finance has been secured.

CONCLUSIONS

The end-product of a bacterial mutagenicity assay does not demonstrate conclusively that the agents involved are carcinogenic. It must be emphasised that demonstration of bacterial mutagenesis is not a demonstration of hazard to human health. In many respects these assays may be regarded as over-sensitive; but their use as a preliminary test to elucidate the presence of potentially hazardous materials, should not be overlooked. Indeed a three-tier approach has been proposed. The first tier would comprise these short term screening tests, the second tier longer term confirmatory tests with whole animals and the third tier would involve a risk-benefit evaluation which may entail further more specialised testing procedures and experiments on the detailed metabolism of the agent *in vivo*. In such a scheme bacterial assays would be invaluable as a rapid, inexpensive early warning system.

The growing importance attached to mutagens in the aqueous environment is illustrated by the fact that the International Standards Organisation (ISO) is at present considering standard methods for the mutagenicity testing of water samples. This action is considered premature in some quarters as a full appraisal of the system available has not yet been made. Mutagens in drinking water must be of paramount importance and these may be naturally occurring, associated with industrial or domestic or agricultural discharges, and may also be produced in the course of water treatment. When more information is obtained as to the nature of these mutagens it would seem highly desirable to commence a programme of elimination. In the future, mutagen testing may be applied a) to a quality criterion for water sources, b) to trace mutagens in water back to source and thereby allow an elimination programme to commence, c) to assess the role of treatment in mutagen production. As some treatment processes (e.g. chlorination) may give rise to mutagens, the role of mutagen testing would have an important role to play in the consideration of an alternative treatment. The study of mutagenesis in the aqueous environment is very much in its infancy but, as more work is completed, it will almost certainly be shown to be an important water quality criterion in terms of human health.

REFERENCES

Ames, B.N. 1973. Carcinogens are mutagens. *Environmental Health Perspectives,* 115-118.

Ames, B.N., Lee, F.D., Durston, W.E. 1973. An improved bacterial test system for the detection and classification of mutagens and carcinogens. *Proceedings of the National Academy of Sciences, USA,* 70, 782.

Kuzma, R.J., Kuzma, C.M. and Buchner, C.R. 1977. Ohio drinking water source and cancer. *American Journal of Public Health,* 67, 725.

Lewin, R. 1976. Cancer hazards in the environment. *New Scientist,* 69, 168-169.

MacLean, M. 1979. Screening for environmental mutagens using the mussel - *Mytilus edulis.* *B.Sc. Honours Project,* Paisley College of Technology.

Page, T., Harris, R.H. and Epstein, S.S. 1976. Drinking water and cancer mortality in Louisiana. *Science,* 193, 55.

Shackleford, W.M. and Keith, L.H. 1976. Frequency of organic compounds identified in water. *Reports from Environmental Research Laboratory,* EPA, Athen Ga.

Simmons, V.F. et al., 1977. Mutagenic activity of chemicals identified in drinking water. *Progress in Genetic Toxicology.* Scott, D., Bridges, B.A. and Sobels, F.H. (eds).

Tye, R.J. and Waite, W.M. 1980. Some practical experiences of mutagenicity testing in the Water Industry. *Proc. 5th Microbiology Seminar.* North West Water, 26.

Discussant's Comments

Andrew Boddy

An appreciation that man's experience of disease can vary from place
to place and be influenced by the environmental characteristics of
these places is almost as old as our awareness of disease entities
themselves. Hippocrates wrote of 'airs, waters and places' and the
governments of cities in renaissance Italy based their attempts at
the control of epidemics on such an understanding (Cipolla, 1976).
A more structured approach is more properly dated to the early part
of the nineteenth century in Britain, however, when the availability
of data from a systematic census (in 1841), the pressures of population changes consequent on the industrial revolution and the emergence of the public health movement combined to require a coherent
mapping of health and disease in the population. Many of the questions which pre-occupied these early pioneers continue to concern
us today - are cities unhealthy places? - but one of the lessons
learned then and still central to the study of these matters is that
place is often simply an indicator of other environmental attributes.
   In gaining this understanding of the behaviour of disease in
populations rather than individuals (and this is the key distinction
between the practice of medicine and the practice of public health),
the Victorians successfully pursued policies of environmental adapt-
ation which did bring under control the important causes of mortality.
One should be clear that it was changes in diet, in housing and in
sanitation and not the therapeutic efforts of the medical profession
that brought about the substantial improvements in health we assoc-
iate with the early part of this century (McKeown, 1965). It is
also worth recalling that the legacy of these policies is the continued monitoring of disease, exemplified by Milne's paper, in which
the 'geographical dimension' continues to play an important part.
   A recollection of this history is necessary if one is to have a
proper perspective of the issues raised by Howe. In the opening
sections of his paper he identifies two, or perhaps three, aspects
of our contemporary society that confuse and complicate our understanding of what should be the late twentieth century analogue of
the Victorian public health movement. The first of these is what
does or does not constitute 'disease' or ill-health and the extent
to which today's problems are properly matters for intervention at
the level of social policy. Howe is right to argue that health is
not simply an absence of disease but it was Rene Dubos who argued
many years ago that health is a mirage. Man's adaption to his environment is, of necessity, an imperfect process; as we improve the
environment, we also recognise and attempt to correct the health
problems that are a consequence of these adaptations (Dubos, 1965).
The epidemic of tuberculosis which lasted for a century in Scotland
is now history and we concern ourselves with the implications for
health of tobacco and alcohol and not housing and diet. In the
1930s, infant mortality rates of the order of ten per cent were not

uncommon; today, we expend substantially greater resources in attempting to reduce a rate of one per cent. What this means is that our ideas about what is health - and what is unacceptable ill-health - are continually changing. As the hazards of the physical environment diminish our focus has turned increasingly towards problems that are inherent in the lifestyle of the individual and the risks to health that are inherent in the social environments we create whether these are new housing estates or the economic decline of the inner city. In the nineteenth century, the public health movement was able to construct an effective model of the relationship between the physical environment and health and to base social policies on it. In our own time, the model of the social environment and its consequences for health is at best imperfect. While it is possible to propose some remedies - such as the control of cigarette smoking - the wider questions of the way in which inequalities in health persist and the way that social conditions contribute to contemporary forms of ill-health are poorly understood.

Howe is also right in his identification of some of the reasons why this might be so. One of the legacies of the nineteenth century was the idea of causative mechanisms of disease - the 'medical model' - which has led to the often inappropriate search for specific causes for diseases (such as coronary artery disease) in ways that are descended from the search for specific infecting organisms in (say) tuberculosis. In some contexts this may not be inappropriate but it had had a distorting - and 'medicalising' - effect on our perceptions of ill-health. In particular, it emphasises illness in the individual and distracts attention from the ill-health of populations or sub-groups of them. This is the second issue identified by Howe and the third - his strictures about the National Health Service - is perhaps simply a consequence of the second experienced at the level of the whole society. Whatever its name, the National Health Service is scarcely about health; it is, instead, a collective approach to the provision of medical care and as such it is powerful and does exercise a substantial influence on the way that our social resources in this field are deployed. In the context of this debate, perhaps one of its effects has been to pre-empt the territory that public health (in its nineteenth century sense) might have occupied.

The issues are not, of course as simple as this brief sketch might suggest. It is perhaps naive to suggest that the medical profession is consciously forcing its view of disease and its alleviation on society; it would be more correct to acknowledge that medicine is primarily about the treatment of disease in the individual so that the medical response to matters of health will inevitably derive from this perspective. Even if, as Howe comments, such perspectives are beginning to change and an interest in 'prevention' is growing, these initiatives (seen, for example, in the health education movement) still focus on attempts to modify the lifestyle of the individual and are thus a development of individual practice. There is little evidence of policies outwith the National Health Service - for example, in respect of food and the content of the national diet - which one could argue were concerned to improve or promote health. Policy is, instead, essentially *laissez faire* and limited to ensuring that diet is 'safe' in the sense of controlling food additives. Similar arguments apply to the regulation of alcohol and tobacco. But nor is this a simple matter; what one might identify as contemporary problems of public health - heart disease, mental illness, alcoholism - are bound up with both the social environment and with individual life-styles within that environment so that action to overcome them will, to some extent at least, involve an intrusion into the life-styles of some people. At the same time, given an environmental component to these problems, it is scarcely surprising that inequalities in health persist and that the geographical patterns of such inequality that were evident in the nineteenth century are still discernable today.

The single group of diseases which best illustrates this present mixture of individual and environmental hazards is the cancers. Some, such as carcinoma of the lung, are largely confined to activities of the individual - in this instance, tobacco smoking. A wide range of others have fairly well recognised occupational origins (the relationship between asbestos and mesothelioma being a typical example) while others - including, perhaps, colonic and rectal tumours - have a less precise environmental content (Doll and Peto, 1981). Geographical studies have played an important part in identifying differences in the cancer experience of populations and thus not only suggesting mechanisms for the causation of individual cancers but also adding to our appreciation of the behaviour of these diseases as a whole and the development of larger models of causation As environments become more elaborate and include new physical components such as complex chemicals, then the arguments for careful monitoring of environmental change become stronger. To some extent this can be done by observing disease itself and the ways in which the pattern changes and this is an appropriate method for - say - many infectious diseases. In the example of cancer, however, the time-scales involved may be very long so that the methods described by Milne become important techniques for the early recognition of new hazards. It will be evident from his paper that the evolution of some of these 'early warning' procedures is at a fairly early and perhaps imprecise stage but this should not diminish the continuing need to monitor the physical environment and to improve the sophistication of the techniques we employ.

Change in the social environment is, of course, a much more complex affair so that, while one would not dispute the differences in measures of health or health outcomes within different parts of large conurbations to which Stewart refers, it is important also to register dissent from the explanations he proposes and the solutions he offers. Geographers will not need to be reminded of the need to understand cities or regions as a complex, interactive whole and this is a view which applies to health as much as to other aspects of life. It is necessary, too, to recall that most measures of health are comparative - so that most will be greater or less than others although often seeming greater when expressed as comparative rates than when viewed as absolute numbers. One might comment also that Glasgow's health is very largely the same as that of other British conurbations; by some measures (perinatal mortality is one) it is probably better. Aspects of recent history such as post-war housing policies have meant that the geography of many cities closely reflects its social structure and thus puts inequalities in health into sharp relief. But these problems are still a reflection of the characteristics of the larger society. They may be reinforced or accentuated by the circumstances of life in large peripheral housing estates but it is dangerous nonsense to suggest - as Stewart does - that the health problems of such areas arise from a state of mind which requires 'psychological disinfection'.

Stewart's argument appears to derive - although very one-sidedly - from a debate which first arose in the United States in the 1960s and which was later expressed by Sir Keith Joseph. This concerned the existence or otherwise of a 'culture of poverty' which distinguished the behaviour of the poor from that of the social main-stream. In Britain, Joseph re-stated the issue in terms of 'cycles of deprivation' and initiated a very substantial enquiry into the whole area under the auspices of the Social Science Research Council. Space does not permit elaboration of the complex questions raised by this proposition; it will be sufficient to say that the research has done much to elucidate the inter-relationship between poverty, behaviour and health but it has failed entirely to demonstrate either 'a culture' of poverty or the kind of psychological infection on which

Stewart bases his argument.

The reality of urban poverty and health is very much more complex. As in other cities, economic change creates poverty and may affect those with uncertain health more harshly than others; demographic trends - and particularly the growth in the numbers of elderly people - have an influence on both the experience of poverty and on health. Changing social assumptions and values (for example, single parent families) may both influence the characteristics of those who 'are poor' and the particular health problems they experience. Other socially vulnerable groups - for example, immigrants - may also contribute in other ways to our overall appreciation of both urban poverty and health. In the last analysis, it is only arguably the case that the individual is wholly responsible for his own well-being; no man is an island and to argue that an individual's health is 'largely a personal responsibility from childhood onward' is to ignore a tradition of scientific research which has consistently demonstrated the opposite view for well over a century.

The real nub of this argument is found in the later passages of Howe's paper. By whatever process, we have lost a tradition which allowed that health - as he uses the word - is a part of the wider agenda of social policy; it has become, instead, a matter of service or professional intervention and is thus focussed on the individual. In the language of another discipline, one might argue that this is a failure of the public health movement to shift its concerns from the physical to the social environment and to maintain its involvement with social policy - the NHS rules OK. Constructing a model of this social environment is scarcely a simple task and it is one that, of necessity, involves a range of disciplines. Improving both the health of the individual and the health of the public requires that we change our perspectives and begin to do so immediately.

REFERENCES

Cipolla, C.M. 1976. *Public Health and the Medical Profession in the Renaissance*. (Cambridge University Press).

McKeown, T. 1965. *Medicine in Modern Society*. (George Allen and Unwin, London).

Dubos, R. 1965. *Man Adapting*. (Yale University Press, New Haven).

Doll, R. and Peto, R. 1981. *The Causes of Cancer*. (Oxford University Press).